THE FLETCHER SCHOOL OF LAW AND DIPLOMACY
A Graduate School of International Affairs
Administered with the Cooperation of Harvard University
TUFTS UNIVERSITY · MEDFORD, MASSACHUSETTS

POWER and DIPLOMACY

THE WILLIAM L. CLAYTON LECTURES
ON INTERNATIONAL ECONOMIC
AFFAIRS AND FOREIGN POLICY

POWER and DIPLOMACY

By Dean Acheson —————————————

HARVARD UNIVERSITY PRESS
CAMBRIDGE, MASSACHUSETTS · 1958

E
835
A25

88902

Library of Congress Catalogue Card Number 58–7135
Printed in the United States of America

The William L. Clayton Lectures

The William L. Clayton Center for International Economic Affairs was established in 1952 at the Fletcher School of Law and Diplomacy in honor and recognition of Mr. Clayton's services as one of the country's leading business-statesmen and its first Under Secretary of State for Economic Affairs. Mr. Clayton is founder and retired head of Anderson, Clayton & Company, the world's largest cotton merchants. His public service includes the following offices: Assistant Secretary of Commerce, 1942–44; Administrator of the Surplus War Property Administration; Assistant Secretary of State, 1944–46; and Under Secretary of State for Economic Affairs, 1946–48.

The foundation of the William L. Clayton Center was officially sponsored by the American Cotton Shippers Association honoring "the accomplishments of Mr. Clayton both in the international cotton trade and as a public servant in the field of economic diplomacy," and "as a means of recognizing his substantial service to the Nation and extending the influence of his example in the field of international trade and diplomacy." Some two hundred individuals, business firms, banks and foundations — principally connected with the cotton trade — joined in contributing the endowment for the Clayton Center.

The program of the Clayton Center — devoted to education and research — includes the William L. Clayton Professorship of International Economic Affairs, a program of research and current policy studies, a program of Clayton Fellowships to encourage and assist outstanding young men and women to prepare for careers in international economic affairs and diplomacy, and the annual Clayton Lectures by persons distinguished in the field of diplomacy, trade or scholarship in international affairs. The Clayton Lectures were inaugurated by former Secretary of State Dean Acheson, in October, 1957, which also marked the opening of the twenty-fifth year of the Fletcher School of Law and Diplomacy.

v

PREFACE

Both the stimulus and the opportunity to write this book I owe to two friends and former colleagues — Mr. William L. Clayton, former Under Secretary of State for Economic Affairs, and Dean Robert Burgess Stewart of the Fletcher School of Law and Diplomacy. Dean Stewart invited me to inaugurate lectures established in honor of Mr. Clayton at the Fletcher School. To do so gave me a welcome opportunity to express my respect and admiration for these friends.

In preparing this volume I have ventured into fields in which the layman must seek, and be profoundly grateful for, the guidance and criticism of the expert and the scholar. I am greatly in the debt of Brigadier General Sidney F. Giffin, USAF, and Mr. W. W. Kaufmann for the elimination of much error, though perhaps they will believe that they have not wholly succeeded. My former colleagues in the Department of State, Messrs. Paul H. Nitze and C. B. Marshall, have most generously read the manuscript and given me invaluable suggestions. Miss Barbara Evans has, again, as in my earlier volumes, shared

the work of investigation and borne the burden of editing.
I am most grateful to all these friends.

A portion of these chapters has appeared in *Western World*, August, 1957, to the publishers of which, Occident-Western World Company, I also extend my thanks.

November 18, 1957   Dean Acheson

CONTENTS

ix

Contents

POWER and
DIPLOMACY

Power Today:
Its Location, Nature,
and Growth

When his hundred years expire
Then he'll set hisself a-fire
And another from his ashes rise
most beautiful to see!
              Alfred Noyes.

To the diplomatist, immersed in the infinite complexity
of daily detail, the most exasperating of questions is one
of the commonest. It comes to him from the inquiring reporter, the Olympian editor, the ironical legislator, the
harassed citizen. What is *the* foreign policy of the United
States? If only they would make it plural, he sighs, how
much more understanding the question would be. He re-
sents, as does every tactician, questions about strategy;
and, as does every strategist, questions about the object
of strategy. Yet, whatever the motive of the question, it is
a good one. It requires him to face his problems, to epit-
omize and declare his line of action.

1

Years ago, when I found myself overwhelmed by detail in preparing for an argument in the Supreme Court, I would summon up the severe Roman countenance of Mr. Justice McReynolds, as he aroused himself from reverie in the midst of my argument to ask, "Counselor, what is this case all about?" The brutal directness of the question brought one up with a start, like a highwayman's "Stand and deliver!" It demanded the heart of the matter without the garnishment of rhetoric.

What is the foreign policy of the United States? It is, I suppose, the grand strategy with which the United States proposes to deal with the main facts — the thrusts and problems they present — of the outside world. It is something which must, in the broadest way, change with the changes in the world around us. There have been times in our history — long times — when there have been few changes, and the world outside our boundaries has seemed very distant and unimportant. But in my lifetime all this has changed. In the first half of this century the world into which I was born has been destroyed. The second half will see what will replace it.

By the middle of the century three major developments had occurred, whose full effect we are now feeling:

1. The decline and, in some cases, the disappearance of the great empires of Western Europe and of Japan; and the emergence of the pre-eminent power of the United States and the Soviet Union;

2. The discovery by man in nuclear weapons of an instrument of unlimited violence; and

3. The Afro-Asian revolution against alien control, and the related revolution of rising popular expectations.

Here were upheavals as revolutionary and far-reaching as any in human affairs. The foreign policy of the United States must be moulded and conditioned to meet them. That policy must be to accept the leadership and laboring oar — in default of any other nation which can do so — in creating a workable system of free states, with the military force necessary to protect them, with the arrangements necessary for their economic development, and with sufficient community of ideas and purposes for their political cohesion.

It is the purpose of this book to show that this can be done, and something of what is necessary to do it.

The Collapse of a World Order

Before the present century was two decades old, the system which had provided an international order since Waterloo was mortally stricken. Twenty years later, it had disappeared altogether.

It is true that in the rosy light of retrospect the period after the Congress of Vienna has seemed more peaceful and idyllic than it was. To the men of the time, says a more realistic writer, the period "was one of appalling turmoil. It was an armed peace. Austria's budget, for instance, was so overburdened by expenditure on armaments that it only once avoided a deficit between 1812 and 1848. France was not pacified: on the contrary resentment against the

3

settlement dominated French political life for a generation. The discontent in the victorious countries was almost as great, except where held down — as in Austria — by police tyranny." [1]

All this is true. Nonetheless, the "Concert of Europe" describes a method and a reality. The empires of Europe, controlling hundreds of millions of people in Europe, Asia, and Africa, and decisively affecting the conduct of hundreds of millions more, did keep international conflict limited in scope and minimal in destruction. They did provide an economic system, accepted without protest, and they did establish political coherence unequaled in extent since the Roman Empire. One essential element in all of this was Great Britain's skillful employment of its power to give stability through shifts of its weight from one side to another, much as a gyroscope gives balance to a moving craft. Another essential element was the managerial and material contribution to economic development, first, by British and, later, by Western European industry and finance.

The First World War ended the Austro-Hungarian, German, and Ottoman Empires and the Czarist regime in Russia, unloosed nationalism in Eastern Europe, and gravely weakened the French and British Empires. The Second World War eliminated the empires of Japan and Italy, and the military power of Germany. France, defeated and occupied, lost her position in the Near East and Far East, and only with increasing difficulty main-

[1] *Times Literary Supplement* (London), April 26, 1957.

4

tains herself in Africa, at the expense of power in Europe. Great Britain, economically exhausted and, save for the African colonies, politically and militarily reduced to her island resources, has by her recent budget decision made clear that the security of the United Kingdom lies in association with other states, and by concentrating military effort in the nuclear field has sought a means of influencing the decision of the United States to fight should Britain's survival be at stake.[2]

The curtain had been rung down upon an era; the stage set for the unfolding of another, which Alexis de Tocqueville, with amazing vision, forecast almost a century and a quarter ago, in his *Democracy in America:*

"There are at the present time two great nations in the world, which started from different points, but seem to tend towards the same end. I allude to the Russians and the Americans. Both of them have grown up unnoticed; and while the attention of mankind was directed elsewhere, they have suddenly placed themselves in the front rank among the nations, and the world learned their existence and their greatness at almost the same time.

"All other nations seem to have nearly reached their natural limits, and they have only to maintain their power; but these are still in the act of growth. All the others have stopped, or continue to advance with extreme difficulty; these alone are proceeding with ease and celerity along a path to which no limit can be perceived. The American struggles against the obstacles that nature opposes to him;

[2] For further discussion of this point, see pp. 60–62.

the adversaries of the Russian are men. The former combats the wilderness and savage life; the latter, civilization with all its arms. The conquests of the American are therefore gained by the plowshare; those of the Russian by the sword. The Anglo-American relies upon personal interest to accomplish his ends and gives free scope to the unguided strength and common sense of the people; the Russian centers all the authority of society in a single arm. The principal instrument of the former is freedom; of the latter, servitude. Their starting-point is different and their courses are not the same; yet each of them seems marked out by the will of Heaven to sway the destinies of half the globe." [3]

Today even the component elements of the world order which had swayed the destinies of the entire globe have been destroyed; beginnings have been made on two alignments to succeed it.

In one of these alignments, Britain, which once had the training and capability to manage a world system, no longer has the capability. The United States, which has the material capability, lacks the experience and the discipline needed for responsible management. This is said in no spirit of belittling those far-reaching, bold, and imaginative steps which this government and people have taken to stop the disintegration of international society and to build anew. Americans, like all sensible people who have had the good fortune to be spared the de-

[3] Alexis de Tocqueville, *Democracy in America* (Alfred A. Knopf, New York, 1945), I, 434.

6

sire for expansion abroad and the experience of national catastrophe from foreign attack, are primarily interested in their own absorbing and immensely profitable affairs, and only secondarily interested in the doings and business of distant peoples. To understand the bearing and urgency of these takes time and experience.

The disappearance of a world system and of the power which sustained it, together with the growth of Soviet power and ambitions, means that the nations which wish to preserve independent national identity can do so only if the material strength and the political and economic leadership of the United States are enlisted in the effort. However much all of us may dislike this thought, the requisite power does not reside anywhere else.

Europe, however, remains of great importance. Its population is still the largest aggregation of skilled workers in the world, its resources are many and varied. Its industry is second only to our own, though closely pressed in many fields by the Russians. Its traditions of civilization go back through two and a half millennia. If Europe should, by evil chance, become subject to Soviet domination, the problems of the remainder of the non-communist world would become unmanageable.[4] The agreement and

---

[4] " . . . Were the United States to stand alone against a Communist world which contained all Europe and the Soviet Union, its 1953 production of 102 million metric tons of crude steel would be outweighed by the Communist 113 million metric tons. Our theoretical capacity (112.7 million metric tons at January 1, 1954) would, however, be equal to that production total. By 1960, ignoring the changes in policy and effort that would obviously take place, our

7

support of Western European nations are necessary for
any successful foreign policy and defense arrangement on
our part. One must not discount the importance of Europe.
But the fact remains that Europe without American
strength and leadership can neither preserve its own independence nor foster an international system in which anyone's independence will survive.

Growth of Russian Power

In the other alignment, Russian power, which has for
two centuries been great, appears to be towering now. In
part this is so because it stands out like a great tree in a
forest where all around it have been felled; in part, because
it has fed on the surrounding decay, and grown. In the

---

anticipated production of 117 million metric tons would be faced
by a combined production of 161.5 million metric tons. That is to
say, our production now would equal 90 percent of the combined
output of our opponents and in 1960 only 72 percent." — *Trends
in Economic Growth, A Comparison of the Western Powers and
the Soviet Bloc*, prepared for the Joint Committee on the Economic
Report by the Legislative Reference Service of the Library of
Congress, 83 Cong., 2 Sess., January 3, 1955 (Government Printing Office, Washington, 1955), p. 140.

The impact of this is even greater if it is true, as the subsequent
JEC Report believes it is, that "The bulk of it [steel] — perhaps as
much steel as in the United States — is available for production of
military goods or for items conducive to further economic growth.
The same kind of comparisons might be made for petroleum."
Soviet Economic Growth: A Comparison with the United States,
prepared for the Subcommittee on Foreign Economic Policy of the
Joint Economic Committee by the Legislative Reference Service of
the Library of Congress, 85 Cong., 1 Sess., July 5, 1957 (Government Printing Office, Washington, 1957), pp. 11–12.

8

past Russian strength lay in its vast area and its large and disciplined manpower. The Soviet regime has added to these assets industrial productive power, which is today the indispensable basis of military power, economic penetration, and political attraction. The Soviet regime gives first importance to its own perpetuation. A strong second effort goes to keeping confusion and unrest as widespread as possible outside the communist area, and to frustrating all attempts to build an international system other than a communist one. All this paves the way for the inevitable — so the regime believes — collapse of capitalistic governments and systems, and for the hegemony of the Soviet Union in a communist world. The regime's efforts gain immense vigor, subtlety, and — for the West — deep deceptiveness from the fact that the Soviet is a revolutionary society, repudiating the most fundamental postulates of the established order, and is in the grip of an ideology which imbues it with unquestioning confidence in its superiority and its destined progression to triumph and dominion.

No matter how plainly the Russians talk and act, we simply refuse to believe what they say and to understand the meaning of what they do. President Eisenhower and Secretary Dulles keep insisting that the test must be deeds, not words. Floods of deeds follow, amply explained by torrents of words. Yet our leaders and, indeed, our people cannot believe what they see and hear.

As I write, President Eisenhower tells us that relations between the United States and the Soviet Union might be improved by a visit from Marshal Zhukov. The President recalls that he and the Marshal "had a most satisfactory acquaintanceship and friendship," and remembers having had "a very tough time trying to defend our position" against the Marshal's contention "that their system appealed to the idealistic, and we completely to the materialistic." [5] The President seems to forget that the same satisfactory friend and persuasive debater insisted upon and carried out the bloody liquidation of the Hungarian revolt. The friendliness which underlies American life makes it impossible to believe that congeniality can accompany the most profound hostility to ourselves and all we believe. As Justice Holmes correctly observed, candor is the best form of deception.

"People," Mr. Khrushchev told the East German communist leaders in September of 1955 — "People say our smiles are not honest. That is not true. Our smile is real and not artificial. But if anyone believes that our smile means that we have given up the teachings of Marx, Engels and Lenin, they are badly mistaken. Those who are waiting for that to happen can go on waiting until Easter and Whit Monday fall on the same day. . . . We are honest people and always tell our opponents the truth. We are supporters of peaceful coexistence but also of education for communism. We are supporters of peaceful coexistence only because there happen to be two systems. We do not need a war to ensure the victory of

[5] *New York Times,* July 18, 1957.

socialism. Peaceful competition itself is enough . . . one cannot stop the course of history."

The object of competition, Khrushchev points out, is the triumph of the Soviet system. He does not *"need"* a war to ensure this victory; but he would quite clearly not reject force if the risks were low, or if, as in Hungary, he felt that the deepest interests of the regime were at stake. Despite all this, we go on seeing in each new move of the Kremlin to divide and weaken us signs that the Russians may at last be "sincere." The very word shows our lack of understanding. The Russians are and have been wholly sincere in what they believe and are pursuing. But their moves and proposals in dealing with other states are coldly and carefully calculated to advance their own purposes, not any common purpose with the West. In this context "sincerity" is a silly and, indeed, a very dangerous word.

Russian industrial production has been growing at a rate as fast as that of any society of which we have record, and greater than most.[6] The technical competence and quality of their heavy industry is no less impressive. For a decade after the Bolshevik revolution in 1917, the period of the consolidation of power, Soviet industry did not equal production under the Czarist regime. This was achieved in 1926; and pre-war production was surpassed

[6] As might be expected, Soviet economic growth has been carefully studied in the United States. What is said here is taken from *Soviet Economic Growth: A Comparison with the United States,* and *Trends in Economic Growth, A Comparison of the Western Powers and the Soviet Bloc,* cited above, note 4.

in 1928. In the ten years from 1938 to 1948 industrial growth was suspended by the Second World War, preparing for it and recovering from it — a period in which United States production increased enormously; steel production, for instance, by a third. So the Russian achievement has taken place during twenty productive years.

In 1928 their production was a little less than ours at the turn of the century.[7] In 1955,[8] within sixteen working years, its was comparable to ours in 1928.[9] In the interval, again taking steel production for comparison, the Soviets increased theirs twelvefold; that of the United States has doubled. In 1955 theirs amounted to 43 per cent of ours. In 1960, so the earlier report to Congress estimates, it will be 51 per cent. But the later report also warns that these figures underestimate the relative power of the Soviet Union where "only an insignificant proportion of that steel goes into satisfying consumer needs for automobiles, washing machines, refrigerators, etc. The bulk of it — perhaps as much steel as in the United States — is available for production of military goods or for items conducive to further economic growth." [10]

In 1928 in Russia "the state of technology was generally backward, and labor skilled in modern technology

[7] *Soviet Economic Growth: A Comparison with the United States*, p. 5.
[8] The last year of reported figures available to me.
[9] *Soviet Economic Growth: A Comparison with the United States*, pp. 23, 36.
[10] *Id.*, p. 11.

12

was scarce." [11] Two years ago the Soviet Union produced more than twice as many bachelors of science as the United States and over two and a half times as many engineers.

This astonishing growth is not hard to understand. It flows from the nature of Soviet society and the time in history when this growth is taking place. By forcing deprivation on the Russian people, the dictatorship has been able since the last war to invest up to 40 per cent of production in capital equipment and arms. In the United States the comparable figure has varied from 25 per cent to 30 per cent. Civilians in the Soviet Union have been permitted to consume only about 56 per cent, while personal consumption in 1956 was 72 per cent of production in France, 70 per cent in Italy, 69 per cent in Canada, 67 per cent in the United States. In Germany, significantly, it was 61 per cent. Then, too, because of the stage of technical development in which this capital investment is being made, Russia has been able to jump from a peasant society to automation without the decades of slow progression through which the Western World had to go in the nineteenth century.

This high rate of growth, so the economists tell us, will tend to taper off as Soviet economy reaches a better balance among industrial equipment, population, and resources. Yet I should stress two factors that are likely to upset the economists' predictions. One is the capacity of

[11] *Id.*, p. 3.

13

the regime to restrict the percentage of production which will go to popular consumption to a level below that of the West; the other, the continued and rapid development of automation in industry.

Automation in industry requires large captial investment, which, in turn, requires continuous increase in productivity and savings. For instance, the Ford Motor Company is replacing most of the expensive machines in its Cleveland engine plant with improved ones. This plant, when it was opened in 1951, was a marvel of automation. But in recent months productivity in the United States has been losing ground to more rapid wage and other cost increases. Working hours have been steadily reduced and the claim for reduction is no longer based on grounds of hygiene. The Twentieth Century Fund "on the basis of increased productivity plus the proportion of gains which the American people have in the past given to time off as opposed to more goods, has estimated that the four-day week will be established by 1975. Meanwhile vacations have been extended. A decade ago there were 34 million weeks taken by the working force; the figure is now calculated to be 70 million." [12]

All this suggests that a most important factor in determining the relation between American and Soviet productive power over the next two or three decades may be the amount of work the people of the opposing social

[12] August Heckscher, "Coming Changes in American Life," Address before the National Conference on Higher Education, Chicago, March 3, 1957.

14

systems may be willing to do and what they make. It is quite possible that the rate at which Soviet production is overtaking ours may not slow down as some have expected. For automation in a society in which civilian consumption is severely restricted can have the effect of increasing considerably the savings available for investment in new productive capacity, which in turn could be even more productive. In another society, where automation might be used to increase consumption and leisure, it could check the development of basic industrial productivity and decrease the relative power of the society.

At all events, regardless of whether Americans continue to be as hard-working as they are now, present trends and common prudence require us to base policy on the hypothesis that, in the absence of a new and vigorous effort on our part, Soviet productive power will approximate that of the United States well before this century is over. Certainly, Mr. Khrushchev is making his plans on that basis. In his Leningrad speech broadcast by the Moscow radio last July he referred to the reorganization of industry and added: "With the improved organization of industrial and building management, with the more skillful use of all the advantages and possibilities of socialist economy we shall be able in a not-too-distant future to solve the problem of catching up with the United States of America in industrial production per capita of population."[13] And recall that the population of the Soviet Union is larger than that of the United States.

[13] *New York Times,* July 7, 1957. Mr. James Reston, in the

The Need for Greater Power in the Free World

Well, we may say, suppose that Soviet production does become equal to ours, what of it? How does it hurt us economically? From the military point of view, will there be any more wars determined by great industrial potential converted to the production of overwhelming quantities of war material? Won't nuclear attacks destroy industrial capacity, so that the wars of the future will be won or lost by the forces in being at the beginning of the war? Or won't they be limited in area and in the size and nature of forces involved and the type of strategy employed?

We shall see later that there is much sense in these questions. It seems also likely that eventually Russian productive power will approximate ours. Nevertheless, should it do so before a workable and working non-communist world system has been established and has enlisted the loyalty of great sections of the world, a most fundamental shift of power would most certainly occur. The Russians understand the necessity for production in their communist area system, and are making great efforts to provide it. They are quite sure that the competition of "peaceful coexistence," if nothing else, will, as Mr. Khrush-

---

report of his interviews with Mr. Khrushchev in Moscow, cites the following views of Mr. Khrushchev: " . . . in another forty years the Soviet Union would have surpassed the United States in industrial and agricultural production.

"The Communists, he said, would leave the United States far behind in another forty years and the world would be proceeding with seven-league steps along the road Marx, Engels and Lenin had outlined." — *New York Times*, October 8, 1957.

16

chev expressed it, "ensure the victory of socialism." The odds would be overwhelmingly against them if under the leadership of the United States, industrial productive power in the non-communist world were also increased to meet unprecedented calls upon it. These calls will be to furnish a military establishment and weapons system more extensive and varied than now exists; to satisfy expanding internal needs; and, in a magnitude not yet understood, to provide foreign investment for those undeveloped areas which are ready and pressing for capital. To many countries this capital would furnish the only alternative to forced saving in the authoritarian style and to dependence for equipment on Soviet industry.

The growth of Soviet power requires the growth of counter-power among those nations which are not willing to concede Soviet hegemony. With this counter-power the future can be faced with hope and confidence, as well as with a sober appreciation of its dangers. Growth of counter-power is needed in our own country, in other industrially developed nations, and in countries only at the beginning of industrial development. There may be a different reason moving each country which objects to Soviet domination. That is unimportant. There will be great differences in their capacity for industrialization. This is important. For help to industrialize (though not subsidy) should be centered in those areas not willing to accept the hegemony of the Sino-Soviet axis and now capable of industrial advance.

The development of these nations will help in two ways

17

to achieve the long-range purposes we have been discussing. In the developed western countries it will stimulate the growth of basic industries which, as we shall see, are needed to produce the military power to safeguard the non-communist world; and it will stimulate the growth of an operating economic system by which those nations capable of achieving higher standards may do so. Both results are needed for political coherence within the area of the system's operation.

As I have suggested, in the nineteenth century an international system of sorts not only kept the peace for a century but also provided highly successful economic working arrangements. It brought about the industrialization of Europe and of many other parts of the world — our own country, for one. It stimulated production of raw materials and led to a great, though unevenly distributed, rise in the standard of living. This was accomplished by the export of capital, primarily by Great Britain, but also by all of Western Europe.

Professor A. K. Cairncross of the University of Glasgow has written impressively of the magnitude of the effort in the extraordinary half century preceding 1914. He calls it symptomatic of this period "that western Europe had invested abroad almost as much as the entire national wealth of Great Britain, the leading industrial country, and a good deal more than the value of the capital physically located in Great Britain." He goes on to say "that Britain herself had invested abroad about as much as her entire industrial and commercial capital, excluding land,

and that one-tenth of her national income came to her as interest on foreign investments." Translating these conditions into the circumstances of this decade and applying them to the United States, Professor Cairncross says that an equivalent situation "would imply American investments overseas of no less than $600 billion and an annual return on those investments of some $30 billion. . . ." To sharpen the contrast between what is and what was, he points out that in recent years private investment has not exceeded $1 billion a year and adds that "even this total has only been sustained by very large investments undertaken by the American oil companies." Professor Cairncross then tells us that "if the same proportion of American resources were devoted to foreign investment as Britain devoted . . . in 1913, the flow of investment would require to be thirty times as great. The entire Marshall Plan would have to be carried out twice a year." [14] I am not suggesting that anything approaching these amounts is possible or necessary; but that a system for the export of capital, much greater than our present hand-to-mouth efforts, is necessary. The system has been destroyed which

[14] *Home and Foreign Investment 1870–1913* (Cambridge University Press, 1953), p. 3. The Department of Commerce reports the net private investment of the United States for 1956 as $2.8 billion. In an interesting article in the July, 1957, issue of *Foreign Affairs*, Messrs. Emilio G. Collado and Jack F. Bennett suggest that from the point of view of foreign development the figure should be nearly twice as large. This addition comes from the investment abroad, rather than the repatriation, of the foreign earnings of American foreign ventures. This point, while an important one, does not bear on the export of capital here discussed.

19

expanded the power of Western Europe and permitted industrial development in societies in which individual liberty survived. One to replace it will be devised, managed, and largely (but not wholly) financed by the United States; otherwise, it is likely to be provided by the Soviet Union, under circumstances destructive of our own power and of an international environment in which independent and diverse nations may exist and flourish.

In the Soviet Union the major effort has gone into scientific research and the establishment of a heavy industry based on the production of energy and the fabrication of metals. Since Soviet industry is still inadequate to meet the demands upon it, the production of capital equipment for further development and for armaments will still be the central object. In our own country and in Western Europe on the other hand, light industry and service industries are growing rapidly. Automobile production has been sharply checked by the fact that old cars, like old soldiers, never die, and usually take plenty of time in fading away. True, substantial demand is made on heavy industry for plant expansion and replacement, for road, bridge, and throughway construction, for schools, housing, and so on. But a still larger base is needed to carry the military requirements and those of foreign development.

Military needs will, for as long as it is profitable to look ahead, exceed means available from our national production. Problems of priority of need and of allocation in meeting needs will still be with us. But no one can doubt that more needs can be met with less sacrifice if the nation's heavy industry becomes larger. To aid in bringing this about and, also, in advancing a workable international economic system, there is another demand which requires only to be made effective. This is the demand for industrial equipment by countries having the managerial and technical manpower to use it — countries such as India and Brazil. The amount of equipment needed is not impossibly large, but it is large enough to stimulate expansion of industrial productive power in the West, and larger than countries, ready for capital, can finance from their own savings. It is important that they be aided to expand faster than their own savings will permit.

Urgency is added by the third of the major current trends in world affairs, namely, the two revolutions, one of nationalism in former dependencies; the other, of rising expectations in all undeveloped areas. There was a time when these areas were isolated from knowledge that higher standards existed elsewhere. That day has passed, particularly in countries where the level of education and competence has permitted industrialization to begin and where, if the necessary capital were available, industrial progress could proceed more rapidly.

And it must accelerate, for we are not given unlimited time to create an operating economic system for the noncommunist world. Without such a system, there are insufficient ties of economic interest which, together with the attraction of military power and the security which the system would provide, are necessary to political cohesion in the non-communist world.

Foreign investment can provide wider opportunity for use of national energies. This can well enhance pride in national achievement and relieve frustrations among members of the populace now denied opportunity to use their full capabilities and training. This should tend to lessen xenophobia, strengthen social fabric and political stability, and bring new meaning to national independence. Areas outside of and independent of the Soviet system will achieve new industrial productive power — the power which underlies military strength and greatly affects international alignments and political arrangements.

One cannot guarantee all these results. On the other hand, those who insist on basing foreign policy on sure things are likely to end up with no policy at all; the test of success in a foreign policy is whether it turns a desired possibility into a probability. The development of productive power in the non-communist world, with complementary efforts to produce strong military forces and to increase all that makes for political cohesion, is the course most likely to bring about a workable international system and a stable power relationship. The probability of achieving all this, given full endeavor on our part, ranges from fair to excellent.

Problems for a Democracy

For a decade and longer issues of critical and fateful importance for the American people and their government, involving the development of this underlying power, will repeatedly arise and demand decision. At best these questions will be difficult to decide wisely. The great danger is that the people and the government of the United States — those who must, and alone can, bear the responsibility of leadership in half the globe — may not realize that they are deciding them at all. Their preoccupations may conceal destiny from them. Should government be willing to take the easy course, to follow rather than to lead, to play the role which some political leaders have always advocated, the real decisions may be secreted in the interstices of American society. This could be a dramatic illustration of Harold Laski's statement that the real sources of sovereignty are undiscoverable.

Two courses are before us. One course is for the American people to use their vast productive power, along with their own hard work, to maintain their pre-eminence and to fashion a system by which they and all who have the will to do so can emerge strong and free from the period of competitive coexistence, of whatever duration. The other course is for the American people to expend their productive power on an increase in consumption and leisure, leaving the non-communist world leaderless, to drift along as best it can. In the absence of wise, and

23

brave, leadership in Washington, who will decide, and when, and where, to follow the first rather than the second course?

The course we shall follow will be affected by thousands of collective bargaining agreements between unions and management, by hundreds of thousands of decisions by investors as to what they will do with their money, by innumerable decisions regarding the management of credit, the determination of prices, the reinvestment or distribution of corporate funds, by tax legislation and government budgets (and all that lies behind them), in decisions about an amorphous idea, called "foreign aid," which press and politicians mould out of slogans and banalities. The course will be affected by events as seemingly remote as the shifts of industry from one part of the country to another, affecting as this does the beliefs of people, and the response of officeholders toward tariff and other economic policies incompatible with any international system.

Dr. Edwin G. Nourse has described how in our democracy decisions can and have become so fragmented as to be, from the point of view of the society as a whole, as unwilled as a stream of consciousness. In this process the leaders of each segment of the society concentrate upon maintaining their position and prestige by insisting upon the most immediate and short-range interests of their group. Opposing groups find it easier to yield than to fight, upon the tacit understanding that their demands, when made, will be likewise accepted. In this situation government too often looks on helplessly, uttering pious admonitions of restraint to the children at the jam pot, certain to unite all against it should it attempt to interfere. One result of this sort of collective interstitial decision is, as Dr. Nourse writes, "that the real source of inflation in postwar United States has lain in the market place — in the institutions and practices of labor union bargaining and corporation price administration." He points to the "eleven 'rounds' of wage increases and a continuous upward march of prices" since the war, when "both management and labor found themselves in a sellers' market, with money demand tending to outrun physical supply. If management raised prices, labor argued that this gave the companies ability to pay higher wages. If labor boosted wages, management argued that it must recoup higher costs by raising prices." Two devices were invented to help the process along; one, the two-phase escalator clause in wage contracts, by which wage rates would rise with a rise in the cost-of-living index; the other, prices high enough to finance cost of plant betterment and expansion without much recourse to the securities market. Unions forced "maximum wage and fringe gains through the strongest union at the most strategic point in business i.e. strongest demand and highest profit margin and then [used] these gains as a lever throughout the labor market." To all of this, the farmers contributed their formula of " 'parity' prices — that is, if prices of things the farmer has to buy go up, the government must support farm prices at a proportionately higher level. This in turn raises the costs. . . ." And the government helps the process directly by stockpiling metals to support their prices and makes "loans on artificially easy terms to construction projects of various sorts to keep up volume when building trade wages and contractors margins tend to price themselves out of the market." [15]

In all of this process no one decided that inflation was a good thing and a policy to be followed. Only a few were conscious, in the highly purposeful and self-interested actions which all were pursuing, that it was involved at all. Most, so far as they thought of the matter, regarded inflation as they regarded sin; they were against it as something evil which others engaged in. Their own actions were manifestations of free enterprise, which had made the country great. Inflation was something that "they" ought to do something about without inconveniencing anyone, while reducing taxes into the bargain. In such an environment decision becomes a series of interstitial reflexes, something, I presume, like the mechanism which operates a centipede's legs.

So it could be in regard, also, to the myriad decisions which will cumulatively determine whether or not our country becomes what it must be, and does what it must do, if the non-communist world is to be pulled together, held together, and led, still strong and free, through "peaceful competition," or "cold war," warm war, or hot

[15] Dr. Edwin G. Nourse, "Sowing the Seeds of Inflation," Address delivered June 24, 1957, Washington, D.C., to the Conference sponsored by the National Citizens Committee to Curb Inflation.

war, or, perhaps, all of them separately or together. These decisions will be put to us not with the dramatic simplicity with which the thunder of bombs posed the issue at Pearl Harbor. A democracy can seal its fate with a gradualism and apparent inevitability which seems to blind its leaders to the nature of the road ahead, as they were blinded in the years before the Civil War.

If the United States is to array itself with power, and lead in the vitalization of "half the globe," all these subtle and hidden questions have to be faced consciously and sensibly. But decisions on perplexing domestic and international economic problems are only the beginning. They lead to decisions on military matters, which involve our own and our families' deepest emotions and interests, decisions on relations between states and peoples, where the knowledge of the wisest and the restraint of the most self-controlled is inadequate, and the opportunity for ignorant and mischievous action is unlimited.

In matters as obscure and requiring as much restraint as these a democracy is faced with its most difficult problems. Only a few very general observations may be ventured. Our people must solve these problems themselves; solution cannot be forced upon them from above. But they can never do what is necessary until they understand what is necessary, and why; and they never will understand that until their leaders in government, business, and labor are willing to tell them. This takes more courage — and vision too — than most leaders, trained and aspiring to succeed in a special and limited constituency, have at their command. So our hope has to rest on the unusual leader who has the rare combination of qualities which are needed for successful leadership in a democracy, not only courage and common sense, but that blending of persuasiveness and wiliness which can make the unpalatable acceptable. To get as far away as possible from controversial figures — Pericles had these qualities and used them. Even he failed in important moments to see all the consequences, as when he accepted the Peloponnesian War and led Athens into it. The best leaders we can produce will make their mistakes, too.

One result, I think, follows from the line of conduct which seems to me necessary. The community will need more help from government than it is getting at present. There are so many opportunities for special groups to profit at the general expense that we cannot expect concern for the public welfare to be sufficient as the sole restraint upon them. So even though greater government direction could also have harmful consequences which would be hard to prevent, it is, nevertheless, essential.

II

The Military Requirements
of a Free World

> . . . We Spartans . . . . are taught to con-
> sider that the schemes of our enemies are not
> dissimilar to our own. . . . In practice we
> always base our preparations against an en-
> emy on the assumption that his plans are
> good; indeed, it is right to rest our hopes not
> on a belief in his blunders, but on the sound-
> ness of our provisions. Nor ought we to be-
> lieve that there is much difference between
> man and man. . . .   King Archidamus,
>   reported by Thucydides.

> War is much too serious a thing to be left to
> military men.   Talleyrand,
>   quoted by Briand to Lloyd George.

We have discussed the basis of power — political, economic, and military — and concluded that it lay in industrial productivity. We have looked at the growing
industrial power of the Soviet Union, fast overtaking ours,
and at the consequences of this; and we have considered
the need and the problem of expanding heavy industry in

developed and in undeveloped countries outside the iron curtain. We must now turn to military power, much as Americans dislike to think about it. For the most part, they regard military power as morally suspect, using "power politics" as a derogatory term. Yet military power has always been fundamental in the relations between states. Today it is the factor in international relations which in the last decade alone has gone through the most revolutionary change.

War has always caught Americans unprepared, intellectually, emotionally, and materially. Even our own Civil War came as a complete surprise, despite all the talk of the "irrepressible conflict," and left the country in shocked horror at the suddenness with which disaster had engulfed it. Our whole history has seemed to teach us that war is a departure from the normal, which "progress" would eliminate. During our colonial period the struggle among the Dutch, French, Spanish, and British for dominion in North America appeared to the colonists only as their involvement in the dynastic wars of Europe, an involvement which later General Washington and Mr. Jefferson were to urge their fellow countrymen to avoid as the first principle of foreign policy.

For over a century after independence our only war with a major power was with Great Britain in 1812, which she fought rather absent-mindedly during the closing phase of her struggle with Napoleon. Later in the nineteenth century we fought Mexico and Spain. We have tended to deprecate this, and regard it as unfortunate roughness in our appointed task of rounding out a continental domain and tidying up a hemisphere. The hundred years of comparative peace which followed the end of the revolutionary wars in Europe, our own remoteness behind our oceans policed by the British fleet, the Zeitgeist, itself, seemed to have brought us to Tennyson's "Vision of the World," seen as Victoria's long reign began, in which

> ". . . the war-drum throbb'd no longer,
>   and the battle-flags were furl'd
> In the Parliament of man, the Federation
>   of the world.
>
> "There the common sense of most shall hold
>   a fretful realm in awe,
> And the kindly earth shall slumber, lapt
>   in universal law."

About the same time Victor Hugo wrote, "In the twentieth century war will be dead . . ." [1] Little wonder that as that century opened war seemed to us an anachronism which we had outlived.

In July, 1914, the murder at Serajevo was just another Balkan political assassination and soon dropped out of the press. On the 13th no mention of Europe cast a cloud over Secretary McAdoo's glowing economic speech — "We can face the future with absolute confidence." [2] With

[1] *The Future of Man.*
[2] *New York World,* July 13, 1914.

31

news of the Austrian ultimatum and the Serbian rejection
of it a week later, alarming reports came from Europe.
"Hundreds of Americans now here [Berlin] are thunder-
struck at this convincing evidence of the war spirit of
modern Germany." [3] But disbelief kept step with alarm.
On the 27th the *New York Times* declared: "To the rest of
the civilized world [outside Europe] it seems amazing,
almost incredible, that a European war of large proportions should be possible at this time. There has been talk
again and again of such a war, but it has always been
averted." On the 28th, it again said, "That [war] is too
dreadful for imagining, and because it is too dreadful it
cannot happen." The *New York World* agreed: "The stakes
are too enormous, the issue of the game too uncertain, for
civilized Europe, if it is in possession of its senses, to risk
its future well-being at the caprice of military gamblers."
On the same day Austria declared war on Serbia. On the
29th the *New York Times* believed that "Sir Edward Grey,
therefore, can with excellent prospects of success act upon
the Berlin suggestion of a conference to confine the war
within the narrowest possible limits." On August 1st it re-
assured its readers that the eight hundred million people
who might be affected by a war were "protected by the
rules of modern warfare. . . . War provokes savagery, but
a war involving the great Powers would be fought with
due restraint." On the same day Germany declared war on
Russia.

When, in 1914 and in 1939, the impossible occurred, it

[3] *New York Times,* July 27, 1914.

produced an emotional and intellectual paradox. The attitudes formed over the century between Waterloo and Mons flowered in the conviction that war was the most horrendous of crimes for which no punishment inflicted upon the individuals and nations whose "war guilt" was established could be too severe. To prevent this crime from ever occurring again — domestic criminal law never hoped to achieve a similar result — international organizations were set up and the most solemn and sweeping pledges made to enforce peace.

At the same time, an equally unqualified, and quite inconsistent, conception regarding the conduct of war seized possession of our minds — the conception of unlimited objectives and absolute victory. People who regarded themselves as the product of a century and a half of rationalism were seized with a blend of romanticism and brutality. Ideas which in modern history had twice proved to be unendurable returned in the garb of idealism. In the religious wars of the seventeenth century and the republican wars of the late eighteenth, a triumphant idea was to be imposed upon a benighted and evil enemy by unlimited force which should destroy all who would not yield. In neither case was the idea triumphant; but the destruction left little to be desired. In the thirty years of the religious wars a third of the population of Europe perished. This is about the estimated percentage of casualties in a thirty-hour nuclear attack upon the United States with our present lack of any adequate civil defense. In many parts of Europe organized society ceased to exist.

33

For a hundred years after both experiences the vividness of those memories taught nations using force not to put in issue the continued existence of the opposing state. One of them could lose — and lose heavily — but survive, as the France of Louis XIV lost to the England of Marlborough, or as Austria and France lost to Prussia in the nineteenth century.

It was left for the prosaic, the pragmatic, the materialistic western civilization of the twentieth century — and nowhere more than in the United States — to recapture the belief in unlimited objectives and unlimited force to achieve them. Our wars, however they began, rapidly mounted to wars to end war, to destroy the war-lords, to make the world safe for quiet people — "peace-loving" was the phrase used — who wanted to be left alone to do — well, what they were going to do was not clearly discerned, but it was assumed to be nonviolent and beneficent. To accomplish this end the cities and industries of the enemy were destroyed, its economic life throttled, its armed forces hammered into "unconditional surrender," its government dissolved, and its leaders executed as criminals. Force complete, absolute, overpowering, was applied until the enemy's will to resist and capacity to exist as a nation were broken. This was victory.[4]

[4] As I re-read the last three paragraphs, I am afraid that, without a further word, they may be misunderstood. The conception which I am criticizing is that when relations between states pass from the condition called peace to that called war, then unlimited violence can and should accomplish unlimited objectives. I am not arguing against the necessity of some kind of military decision

The triumph of the belief in unlimited force was, in part, the moralism of an outraged pacifism, and, in part, the conclusion of military men entranced by Clausewitz's theory of pure war. Certain American generals became the poor man's Clausewitz, as, for instance, General Mark Clark, before a subcommittee of the Senate Judiciary Committee inquiring into the conduct of the Korean War.

"Once our leaders, our authorized leaders, the President and Congress, decide that fight we must, in my opinion we should fight without any holds barred whatsoever.

"We should fight to win, and we should not go in for a limited war where we put our limited manpower against the unlimited hordes of Communist manpower which they are willing to expend lavishly, and do. . . .

---

when, for instance, international relations and power ratios are permitted to reach the state they reached in 1939.

Probably there was no alternative then to prosecution of the war to a conclusion sufficiently decisive to bring about a change of regime in Berlin and in Tokyo. The Napoleonic wars could be ended only when Waterloo removed Napoleon. But, even then, the ends sought and the methods used by the allies after 1815 were much more limited than after 1945. But my point goes further. Had Britain, France, and the United States commanded in the 1930's the military power, much less than they had in 1945, to stop the Italian attack in Ethiopia and the occupation of Manchuria and the Rhineland, they could, by the limited use of force for a limited purpose, have preserved a balance, stability, and restraint in international affairs which we might now envy. They might even have made the world safer against war-lords and for democracy than it now is.

"If fight we must, let's go in there and shoot the works for victory with everything at our disposal." [5]

Unlimited Objectives and Absolute Victory No Longer Possible

General Clark's words no longer have any acceptable meaning in strategy or policy. With the possession of thermonuclear weapons and means for their delivery, with the advent of an intercontinental missile, "victory," in the General's sense of the word, is no longer attainable. The victory which he would gain by shooting "the works . . . with everything at our disposal" is what the General had experienced — a prostrate enemy whose will to resist had been so broken by a rain of destruction that it was wholly amenable to the victor's will. But what responsible official would today expect such a conclusion of unlimited war between nuclear powers?

The responsible maker of policy would be most unwise not to assume that both the United States and the Soviet Union have sufficient nuclear capacity to retaliate with lethal power, whichever might strike first. There is military opinion, greatly to be respected, that the time of complete nuclear stand-off has not yet arrived. This may be right; but to base policy upon it seems to me too dangerous. It should be regarded as a strengthener of

[5] *The Korean War and Related Matters, Report of the Subcommittee to Investigate the Administration of the Internal Security Act and Other Internal Security Laws to the Committee on the Judiciary,* United States Senate, 84 Cong., 1 Sess., January 21, 1955 (Government Printing Office, Washington, 1955), p. 7.

36

resolution in time of crisis. At the time of the attack on South Korea some able and conscientious officers considerably overestimated the capacities of their services. The army estimates were most consistently conservative and nearer right.

The policy maker must also plan, from the nature of the two societies, upon the likelihood that the first blow, if there is to be one, will be struck by the U.S.S.R. How lethal that blow could be has been described by many writers.[6] Without repeating the details of their calculations, it is enough to say that a successful nuclear attack on the United States could result, on conservative estimates, in death or injury to a third of our population. The destruction and disruption of our highly specialized and interdependent society could be so great that the nation, as an operating entity, would either cease to function, or be forced to devote all its efforts to the survival of the living. Since our own retaliatory force should be in the air, or in missile launching stations, when the blow fell, the nation, though gravely — perhaps fatally — wounded, could still launch an equally destructive counter-blow against the enemy. So long as both nations can preserve their retaliatory force through an initial attack, a strategy of unlimited nuclear attack is a strategy of mutual suicide. It becomes one of the highest aims of policy to avoid this disaster.

[6] Most recently, and most clearly for the lay reader, by Mr. Henry A. Kissinger in *Nuclear Weapons and Foreign Policy* (Published for the Council on Foreign Relations by Harper & Brothers, New York, 1957).

The first American reaction to the danger was a typical one. It was to legislate it out of existence, just as we had tried to legislate war out of existence in the Kellogg-Briand Pact. It seemed to many of our leaders in government, church, press, and science that the mere dramatization and repetition of the horrors of nuclear war were enough to "bring them home" to all peoples and lead them to abolish the danger altogether. In the Soviet Union, however, people were carefully isolated from these disturbing thoughts. So far as foreign propaganda is concerned, a communist's home is his castle.

Our predicament has been well described by Mr. Kissinger. From the dawn of legend, Prometheus, who stole the secret of fire from the gods, and in punishment was chained to a rock with a vulture tearing at his liver, has symbolized the penalty of presumptuous ambition. Our generation has stolen the secret of a fire which Prometheus could not imagine, and is doomed to live with the horror of its achievement. There are less metaphysical reasons why we shall not escape with a mere lifetime of penance. Most of those who have thought and worked on the problem of disarmament — though there are men entitled to respect who think otherwise — have come to the conclusion that attempts to agree with the Russians on the control of nuclear energy have ended in frustration for the same reasons that impeded solution of all our other differences. We have too little common ground and purpose with a society dedicated to the destruction of ours to reach any basic agreements requiring mutual trust. But we do have some common ground, the common ground of what Mr. Churchill has called mutual terror. Upon that and upon our own strength and courage it may be possible to bridge the chasm which yawns before us.

During the years in which we had a nuclear monopoly the Russians, through Stockholm peace proposals and other means, vociferously led the propaganda to "ban the bomb" — which was their phrase for halting our nuclear efforts until they caught up. At home they deprecated the importance of these weapons. "Atomic bombs," said Stalin, "are intended to frighten people with weak nerves. . . ." So long as the U.S.S.R. was without an adequate stockpile, its people heard no frightening talk, and the non-communist world was deluged with it. Now that that period is over — a period which Moscow believed to have been one of great danger, as it certainly would have been for us had roles been reversed — Russian propaganda to "ban the bomb" is still good propaganda with the non-nuclear powers. For a decade now East and West have trod the intricate and formalized measures of negotiations to control nuclear energy and armament, from the more far-reaching proposals of 1946 and 1951 to those discussed in London during the current year. It is my conviction that the only agreements which are possible now would be disadvantageous to us and would not diminish the dangers of nuclear war.

So, unpleasant as the conclusion is, we cannot avoid the fact that force will play a great part in the grand strategy of creating a workable non-communist world system.

What tasks, then, may we properly ask our soldiers, sailors, and airmen to be prepared to perform? With what weapons do they perform these tasks? These questions require us to cover familiar ground.

The Function of Force in a
Free World System

The United States does not want military power in order to take what belongs to others, or to make anyone accept its overlordship. We have no dreams of conquest or *pax Americana*. But, unhappily, the possibility always exists that force may be used against us and our interests, or against the interests of our allies, or the interests of other nations whose independence is important to us. Military power is necessary to deter these interferences or, if they do occur, to stop them.

Whatever hopes, or illusions, might have been entertained at the end of war, no one can believe any longer that the military power to protect these interests can be furnished by anyone but ourselves and our allies. The United Nations is only all of us — those who may be using force and those who may be resisting. It can have no force except what its members contribute and support. It has always been plain that the United Nations could not use force against a great power. The veto in the Security Council was put there to prevent the legal questions from ever arising; and, as a practical matter, to attempt it would only bring on a major war. Also, as a practical matter, small nations run little risk of interference by force organized by the United Nations. A dispute is not likely to arise in which the divergent interests of East and West and of the voting blocs would not paralyze military action. Even in the recent Suez situation, where the United States and the Soviet Union seemed to be siding together with large majorities, a United Nations force only acted after the military phases were over and only at the sufferance of the contending parties.

Furthermore, it would be a great and dangerous mistake to mould political or military policy or action out of a fancied necessity of "reconciling" it with the United Nations Charter.

It is true that Article II calls upon all members to settle their disputes by peaceful means and to refrain from force against the territorial integrity or political independence of any state. Whatever these words may mean, we cannot accept from them any limiting obligation not reciprocally accepted by our opponents. The rules must be the same for all. The words in question did not inhibit the part played by the Soviet Union in Korea and Hungary. We cannot permit them to foreclose us from action which we might consider wise and requisite in countering the use of force against us. Whether the force is used on a considerable scale by a great power through a satellite, or whether it is used on a smaller scale by a small power to interfere with vital interests previously recognized and established, the Charter as interpreted by others leaves us free to meet this force as we think best. The Charter may be a factor in determining what we think best; but it can have no more determinative authority with us than it does with others. To regard ourselves as inhibited by its words because we argue unsuccessfully that others should be so governed, or in order to set an example for those who have not the least intention of following it, seems to me a very bad bargain indeed.

The United Nations and its Charter are neither an aid nor an impediment in determining military policy. A sounder guide lies in political and military considerations.[7]

Discussion must contemplate a vast range of violence — at one end, the destruction which one nuclear power may hurl at another; then, the sort of hard and bitter fighting which occurred in Korea; finally, the force which might be used to deny our shipping the use of the Suez Canal. All of this is force which we should be in a position to deter, or, if it is not deterred, to overcome.

Here one must pause to ask what is meant by deterrence. To deter another is to prevent him from doing some-

[7] Dag Hammarskjold, in the Introduction to the Annual Report of the Secretary General of the United Nations, made public September 4, 1957, says: "The events of the past year have, I believe, cast a clearer light upon the role of the United Nations in these times. The Charter, read as a whole, does not endow the United Nations with any of the attributes of a super-state or of a body active outside the framework of decisions of member governments. The United Nations is, rather, an instrument for negotiation among, and to some extent for, governments. It is also an instrument added to the time-honored means of diplomacy for concerting action by governments in support of the goals of the Charter. This is the role the organization has played, sometimes successfully, sometimes with disappointing setbacks, throughout its life." — *New York Times,* September 5, 1957.

thing, by a threat to do him harm under certain circumstances, which he believes we will do and does not want to provoke. "A threat," as I have said before, "is not believed, and therefore cannot deter, unless there is general conviction that the threatener has both the capacity and the intention to carry out the threat. The deterrent to the use or threat of nuclear bombs today is the belief by the initiator that he would receive retribution about as devastating as the attack. . . . [It] will be effective to protect us only as long as it is believed elsewhere that we are maintaining the capacity and the will to launch a crushing nuclear reply if our vital interests are attacked." [8]

To maintain this capacity, and widespread belief in it, requires an effort costly in funds, in technical training, and in inventive genius. Weapons for mass destruction already exist of such power and in such numbers that such practical need as exists to increase either could be met at relatively small cost. But the means of delivery of the weapons are still in the stage of development.

The recent Russian achievements with long-range rockets may well indicate a change, to our disadvantage, in the strategic situation. Clearly they mark serious political and prestige loss for us. But the Russians still remain vulnerable to our retaliatory blows. This, of course, underlines the importance of our overseas bases,[9] and of putting

[8] *A Citizen Looks at Congress* (Harper & Brothers, New York, 1957), p. 120.
[9] The contribution of political policy has been the acquisition of our rights to establish air bases overseas. The value of these is two-

greater effort and funds into the development of delivery systems. This should be, and we are told is,[10] a major aim of military policy. But belief in this is shaken by reports that the amount spent on missile development is arbitrarily restricted to a fixed percentage of the whole military budget; ten per cent is usually mentioned.

The development of nuclear striking power will be of little value unless its survival against surprise attack is insured. Our air force has been created and trained in an atmosphere of offensive strategy. But this can be overdone. This government and people will not — and should not — plan and execute an initial attack on the Soviet Union. This being so, it is all the more necessary that our nuclear striking force must be able to survive a surprise attack against us, and it must be known to be able to do so. This is the very heart of its deterrent effect.

No matter how great our force may be, it will have less

---

fold: they increase and diversify striking power; and they may lengthen the warning time of an attack against us.

[10] President Eisenhower's statement of policy is as follows:

"For a long time, the long-range missile is not going to provide the best means of delivering an explosive charge, and that is all it is for. For a long time, there will be a change-over as they become perfected.

"In our own case, we have spent many, many millions of dollars, as have other nations. We are continuing to do so at a — on what is the highest priority that can possibly be devoted to the capacity of our — of our scientific advancement, and to the capacity of our own, you might say, arrangements and organization to bring the thing forward; that is, testing, plans, and organization and the development, manufacture, and so on. But the big thing to remember is that a mere tested vehicle is a long ways from actual production." — *New York Times,* September 4, 1957.

deterrent effect if it is highly vulnerable to surprise destruction. "Proper preparedness here," writes Brigadier General S. F. Giffin, USAF, "of course demands that an air force be organized, equipped, and deployed so that no enemy attack, however sudden, can deprive it of the retaliatory ability to penetrate enemy defenses and virtually destroy the enemy home base." [11] In the defense of our indispensable striking force far more can and should be done than is being done. The resources and effort which can be well invested here are great indeed — the elaboration and perfection of warning systems, interception defenses by plane and rocket (until the intercontinental rocket arrives), the dispersal of the strategic air command, and so on — all of these are of the highest importance and complexity, particularly when the warning period may well be in the neighborhood of two to three hours. After the intercontinental missile is produced, it may be about fifteen minutes.

The object of military and political policy is to magnify the already formidable difficulties in the way of a nuclear attack upon us, so that the risks of the enterprise may continually — and, if possible, increasingly — outweigh the potential gains. "Deterrence," says Mr. Kissinger, "is the attempt to keep an opponent from adopting a certain course of action by posing risks which will seem to him out of proportion to any gains to be achieved." [12] One in-

---

[11] "A New Future for World War II?" *World Politics*, January, 1957, pp. 280, 283.
[12] Kissinger (cited above, note 6), p. 96.

45

creases the deterrence when one magnifies the risks of destruction which the opponent incurs and decreases the measure of destruction which he may be able to inflict.

This last raises at once the vast and complicated problem of civilian defense. The Congress has steadfastly refused to take the matter seriously; little money has been provided; not even adequate plans have been made. Yet here is action which could have immense deterrent effect. The object is primarily one of saving people; the dangers to plants, though great, are much less. The problem, specifically, is to provide shelters, uncontaminated water and food for periods which may run into several weeks. If by these measures casualties could be reduced to a third or a fifth of what they would be under present circumstances, this could well save the whole national structure from collapse, and make the risks of an attack on us far outweigh the probable gain.

The Limitations of Massive Retaliation as a Deterrent

But the possession of nuclear power will not deter, or stop once it has started, the use of all kinds of force. Deputy Secretary of Defense Quarles has said that "if we have the strength required for global war, we could certainly meet any threat of less magnitude." [13] This simply is not true. It did not prevent the Russian-instigated and sup-

[13] See James E. King, Jr., "Limited Defense," Part I of his review of *Nuclear Weapons and Foreign Policy* in the *New Republic,* July 1, 1957, p. 18.

46

ported attack on South Korea, or the loss of North Viet Nam, or the seizure of the Suez Canal. "Deterrence," says Mr. J. E. King, Jr., ". . . requires a certain proportion. . . ." He stresses that the retaliation which we propose in order to deter actions we consider aggressive must be believable. He particularizes that "an opponent whose purpose is the subversion of Baghdad may find it difficult to believe our claim, for example, that his initiative involves the destruction of Moscow *and New York*." [14]

This forces us back to the essence of deterrence — that the threat shall be credible. To put forward as a policy a threat which is incredible may be to stay within the yet uncharted bounds of permissible fraud in politics, but it is highly dangerous for the country, and utterly destructive of the effort to create a workable non-communist world system. In January, 1954, the Secretary of State unveiled a new foreign and military policy worked out, so he said, by the military and civil authorities and approved in the National Security Council by the President. It is best to let him present its rationale and its content in his own words:

"So long as our basic policy concepts were unclear, our military leaders could not be selective in building our military power. If an enemy could pick his time and place and method of warfare — and if our policy was to remain the traditional one of meeting aggression by direct and local opposition — then we needed to be ready to fight in the Arctic and in the Tropics; in Asia, the Near East, and in

[14] *Id.*, p. 20.

Europe; by sea, by land, and by air; with old weapons and with new weapons. . . .

"But before military planning could be changed, the President and his advisers, as represented by the National Security Council, had to take some basic policy decisions. This has been done. The basic decision was to depend primarily upon a great capacity to retaliate, instantly, by means and at places of our choosing. Now the Department of Defense and the Joint Chiefs of Staff can shape our military establishment to fit what is *our* policy, instead of having to try to be ready to meet the enemy's many choices." [15]

In the ordinary sense of the words used, this statement means that, should force be used against us or our interests in various parts of the world, we would not meet it with

[15] Secretary of State John Foster Dulles, "The Evolution of Foreign Policy," Address before the Council on Foreign Relations, New York, January 12, 1954, *Department of State Bulletin*, January 25, 1954, pp. 107, 108. Vice President Nixon's expression of the doctrine is as follows: "We found that economically their [the Soviet] plan, apparently, was to force the United States to stay armed to the teeth, to be prepared to fight anywhere — anywhere in the world — that they, the men in the Kremlin, chose. Why? Because they knew that this would force us into bankruptcy; that we would destroy our freedom in attempting to defend it.

"Well we decided that we would not fall into these traps. And so we adopted a new principle. And the new principle summed up is this:

"Rather than let the Communists nibble us to death all over the world in little wars we would rely in the future primarily on our massive mobile retaliatory power which we could use in our discretion against the major source of aggression at times and places that we chose." — *New York Times*, March 14, 1954.

"direct and local opposition" — a form of action which would enable us to employ the minimum force required to stop the interference with our interests. Instead, the new policy is to "depend primarily upon a great capacity to retaliate, instantly, by means and at places of our choosing." This calls for dependence on the Strategic Air Command. And where are we to use it? Not, said the Secretary, where an enemy might pick his time and place, not "in the Arctic and in the Tropics; in Asia, the Near East, and in Europe." But we should use it at our own time and "at places of our choosing." If this means anything, it means that we depend upon the Strategic Air Command armed with nuclear weapons to make surprise attacks on an opponent's strategic centers.[16]

[16] In a recent article, "Challenge and Response in United States Policy," *Foreign Affairs,* October, 1957, pp. 25, 31, Mr. Dulles seems to back away from massive retaliation. After referring to his earlier doctrine, he writes: "However, the United States has not been content to rely upon a peace which could be preserved only by a capacity to destroy vast segments of the human race. Such a concept is acceptable only as a last alternative. In recent years there has been no other. But the resourcefulness of those who serve our nation in the field of science and weapon engineering now shows that it is possible to alter the character of nuclear weapons. It seems now that their use need not involve vast destruction and widespread harm to humanity. Recent tests point to the possibility of possessing nuclear weapons the destructiveness and radiation effects of which can be confined substantially to predetermined targets.

"In the future it may thus be feasible to place less reliance upon deterrence of vast retaliatory power. It may be possible to defend countries by nuclear weapons so mobile, or so placed, as to make

Is this a credible threat? Apparently not even those who made it meant it. The first opportunity to employ the threat of massive retaliation came even before the doctrine was formally announced — to end the Chinese intervention in Korea. But the "limited war" was continued until the conclusion of an armistice on the terms sponsored by the United States and adopted December 3, 1952 by resolution of the United Nations General Assembly. Another opportunity came when the fate of Indochina was in the balance in 1954, but that country was divided instead; a third, when the people of Budapest were crushed for rising against Russian tyranny. The retaliation was all one way, and by means and at places chosen by the Kremlin. "Regardless of the actual historical circumstances," Dr. Hans J. Morgenthau has written, "under which the use of force was here averted, there can be little doubt that 'brinkmanship' cannot be practiced indefinitely without challenge, and that must be even more true of what might be called 'open brinkmanship, openly arrived at' — that is, 'brinkmanship' whose deterrent effect is counteracted by retrospective boasts as well as by the official rhetoric of pacifism. Sooner or later someone will want to know

---

military invasion with conventional forces a hazardous attempt. For example, terrain is often such that invasion routes can be decisively dominated by nuclear artillery."

This, of course, is not to pick our own time and to fight "at places of our choosing," but seems to be a reversion to the "traditional [policy] of meeting aggression by direct and local opposition." The only innovation suggested is the tactical use of the smaller nuclear weapons. The soundness of this suggestion is discussed later on in this chapter.

50

whether the statesman approaching the brink is serious or bluffing, whether he will jump or pull back. Then the alternative will be war, or peace by appeasement." [17] Do any of us seriously believe that an American government would take the position that an attack on Quemoy would involve the destruction of Peiping or Moscow, or both, *and of New York?*

The answer is, of course, that the threat is not credible. That unhappily is not the whole answer. We must add to it that, in developing the composition of its military forces, this government has been acting for some years as though it were going to rely upon this incredible threat. As a result other courses are being foreclosed. In the consequent situation our only choice is to do all and to bring on devastation which we may not survive and which the issue cannot justify, or to do nothing and thus to lose position after position without a struggle.

No situation could more readily destroy cohesion between the United States and other states in the non-communist world, for it advertises itself as a prescription for failure. Nor could any situation be more calculated to increase the risk of nuclear disaster resulting from miscalculation by our opponents. Our lack of any effective response except nuclear retaliation will serve only to tempt our opponents to push their incursions and provocations further and further. Our allies will be the first to suffer; our own, by no means phlegmatic, population will soon

[17] "Atomic Force and Foreign Policy," *Commentary*, June, 1957, pp. 501, 504.

be calling for action. There will be many ready to urge, "Let's go in there and shoot the works for victory with everything at our disposal." The best hope of working through the troubles of a deeply divided world in a nuclear age lies in a very considerable degree of rationality among the nuclear powers. A mad man in high places, or one as nearly mad as Hitler, could destroy us all by the error of his calculation of probable risks and gains, and of the probable action of the other side. Here is where the clarity of our intention and of the probable degree of our military action in various contingencies is most important. To keep the opponent guessing may be useful in some fields, but not in this one. For, if he wrongly guesses that we are going to hit him, the likelihood is that we shall be hit ourselves. One of the most dangerous ways to keep our opponents guessing is to keep ourselves guessing. "The dilemma that confronts the Western world today as it contemplates the use of force is only partly the consequence of the unacceptable horror of all-out atomic war," writes Dr. Morgenthau. "In good part, too, it is the consequence of the 'new look' of Western military policy. For what makes it so difficult for the West to contemplate the use of force is its own tendency, created by its new military policy, to identify force with atomic force. Yet the use of atomic force, however narrowly circumscribed by the initial intent, entails the enormous and unbearable risk that it may develop, imperceptibly but ineluctably, into the use of all-out atomic force." [18]

[18] Morgenthau, p. 505.

The truth is that, having sought for a mechanical, painless, and cheap method of deterring the use of all force against us, we have lost sight of the problem. Our present policy rests upon the assumption of a present or attainable significant United States superiority in nuclear weapons. By significant, I mean sufficient superiority so that the gains from all-out nuclear attack are well worth the risk of damage to ourselves. No sensible policy can rest on this assumption. "Between great and competitive powers some approach to military parity is entirely normal, and a disparity such as that which existed during the brief period of the United States atomic monopoly occurs but rarely." [19] In reality, the purpose of our nuclear striking force, the Strategic Air Command, and of all the effort and expense it so richly deserves, is to deter a major attack against us and our allies. Its highest success would be the absence of any occasion for its use. No achievement could more richly reward all the training and devotion of its men and the genius and sacrifice which equipped them. Under the shield of its protection we need other and different forces, which we do not have, to respond to lesser forcible challenges to our interests, to achieve limited objectives, and to make possible and credible our determination, with others, to provide security for a workable noncommunist world system other than by blowing it to pieces.

[19] Giffin (cited above, note 11), p. 285.

What Military Capacity Do We Need Beyond That for Total Nuclear War?

The capacity we need is not to be thought of as merely auxiliary to the Strategic Air Command, or as designed to conduct world war on the model of 1914 or 1940. The forces required have a wholly different function, and should have different equipment, and training. They need all the present military arms — land, sea, and air — high mobility, their own transport, great fire power, and as little as possible of what the Romans called impedimenta. For they may have to fight at short notice in many of the places which the Secretary of State thought undesirable. Their function is to meet "aggression by direct and local opposition." This idea of a separate force for a separate function is fundamental; for those who are concentrated, as they should be, on nuclear striking power and defense cannot be expected to develop the forces needed for limited warfare. They will always regard these forces as a troublesome adjunct to their main preoccupation.

Furthermore, the separateness and complete difference of the forces would underline our intention, in meeting force used against our interests with force, to keep the conflict to a minimum, to achieve the limited purpose of stopping the injury, to pose no threat of massive nuclear attack. This should minimize miscalculation of our intention.

The limited force which we might have to meet with limited response might come from a great power or a

54

small one. It could be organized, supplied, and directed by the U.S.S.R., through a satellite, as a probing action, a test of will, or an attempt to gain an end with minimal risk. The attack on South Korea was of this nature. At one time it seemed possible that a similar probe might be made by other satellites against Yugoslavia, which it would have been both possible and desirable to stop. Or it could be action of a small nation, probably supplied by the U.S.S.R., and encouraged by the belief that apprehension of Russian moves would prevent opposition, such as the military seizure of the Suez Canal, and the threatened overthrow of the Jordan government by Egypt and Syria.

Not all conflicts are mortal challenges, and not all should be made to appear so. It is sometimes argued that limited war, which involves nuclear powers even indirectly, is impossible because each side, rather than lose, would expand the scope and character of the conflict until it would end in mutual nuclear destruction. History and the dictates of common sense deny this dichotomy of destruction or appeasement. Even Admiral Radford's authority will not validate his conclusion: "I think it is pretty generally understood that the United States is not going to allow themselves to be defeated with their best weapons still unused." [20]

The Admiral's use of the word "best" is interesting. It brings us back again to the basic conception of "defeat" and "victory." Victory in limited war is not gained by putting the existence of the opposing state — and our own,

[20] King (cited above, note 13), p. 19.

too — in issue. It does not seek unconditional surrender; it does not necessarily mean attaining all that we desire. The aim of limited war is to stop the infringement upon our interests. If, out of this, can come some gain to the opposing state as well, all the better. It is even conceivable that we might accept being unsuccessful in a limited war with our "best weapons still unused," if by our own "best weapons" is meant all-out nuclear attack.

To accomplish the purpose of a limited war, we must be able to strike fast and hard. Korea and Suez drive home this lesson. We are told that at present, "It would require the entire available United States airlift, including the civil reserve fleet, over thirty days to move one division from the United States to the Middle East, provided all air-transport units were in position when the crisis occurred and provided they were not required for any other mission — two most unlikely contingencies." [21] Even the new greatly lightened and less encumbered airborne division would require the services of the whole airlift for fifteen days, and to lift a regimental combat team to Laos would take it ten days.[22]

The men needed for forces of this sort will require a large percentage of professional soldiers in a high state of readiness, both because of the complexity of the weapons involved, and the morale and training needed to use them under the probable circumstances of the action. Half trained reserves or rapidly rotating draftees will not do.

[21] Kissinger (cited above, note 6), p. 163.
[22] *Ibid.*

As for quantities, General Taylor has placed the Army's needs at twenty-eight modern divisions. We have fifteen, of which not more than twelve could be called combat-ready. Our Army was undermanned in 1950; we paid heavily for it in Korea, which we seem already to have forgotten, as these figures indicate:

Army Strength	Date
660,000	July 1, 1949
593,000	" " 1950
1,532,000	" " 1951
1,596,000	" " 1952
1,534,000	" " 1953
1,404,066	" " 1954
1,108,343	" " 1955
1,024,887	" " 1956
1,000,000	" " 1957

By orders of July 16 and September 19, 1957, Secretary of Defense Wilson directed cuts totalling 200,000 men in the armed services, half of which will come out of the Army. He also announced that a further cut of 100,000 men is under consideration to be decided upon in preparing the budget for the fiscal year beginning July, 1958. This action drew from Mr. Hanson Baldwin the gloomy comment: "But, if [we follow] to its logical conclusion the road upon which we have started, we shall be dependent for defense upon the atom alone; we shall have sacrificed on the altar of economy the capability of fighting non-nuclear wars. The result, if carried to the extreme, could be dollar savings at the cost of national existence." [23]

The Air Force is concentrating the funds at its disposal on the vital task of preparing and maintaining nuclear striking power. I am not suggesting that less — but rather more — is needed for this. The planes and missiles built and building to carry nuclear weapons through intercontinental space would operate inefficiently and be exposed to risk of loss under circumstances of limited warfare. If limitations of our economy left no other alternative, these consequences would, of course, have to be faced. But no such limitations need be accepted and it would be dangerous economy to do so. There will always be disposition on the part of those who design, operate, and control weapons produced for total warfare to reserve them for this extremity, or — if they are used — to use them in the manner for which they were intended. This disposition imposes an undesirable limitation on the air forces most useful for the bombing and support missions of limited war.

Similarly, the Navy — with more questionable judg-

[23] *New York Times,* July 18, 1957. Mr. Baldwin added: "The cuts in manpower, coupled with prior restrictions upon the procurement of transport aircraft, make even more remote the chances of establishing a completely air transportable 'fire brigade' reserve capable of being flown with nuclear and non-nuclear weapons from the United States to any part of the world." The disarmament proposals presented by the Western allies to the Soviet Union in London and published on August 29, 1957, in three steps would reduce the total number of men in the U. S. armed forces — land, sea, and air — to 1,700,000. — *State Department Bulletin,* September 16, 1957, p. 451.

ment — has been heavily weighting its expenditures upon supercarriers as its contribution to total nuclear war. Inevitably the Navy's part in limited war has been given second place. Here the Navy will not be called upon to perform its historic mission of seeking out and destroying the enemy's forces, as did Themistocles at Artemisium and Salamis, Octavian at Actium, Nelson at Copenhagen, the Nile, and Trafalgar, Dewey in Manila Bay, Togo in the Sea of Japan, and Spruance at Midway. Its task will rather be to aid in the transport and supply of troops, to furnish air support, and give protection against a growing submarine menace, which with the development of rockets will be very great to fleets and ports.[24] This very important role it played in European and Pacific landings in the last war.

[24] *The Observer* (London), July 28, 1957, stated that the Soviet Union already has "the greatest submarine fleet in the world — upwards of 500 craft and probably increasing at the rate of eighty a year."

On August 26, 1957, Admiral Arleigh A. Burke, Chief of Naval Operations, USN, told the Veterans of Foreign Wars, "They [the Soviets] have a large, well-rounded navy with the largest submarine force in history, and they are building subs at the rate of about 100 a year." — *New York Times*, August 27, 1957.

"Adm. Jerauld Wright, NATO Atlantic commander-in-chief, said tonight that naval exercises just concluded in the North Atlantic showed his forces had serious shortages and 'deficiencies' in the field of anti-submarine warfare.

"Wright, one of America's top naval leaders, said he agreed with British officers who said NATO's 'Sea Watch' exercise revealed 'grave deficiencies' in Western anti-submarine capabilities. . . .

" 'We have, however, serious shortages in modern devices against submarine attack,' he said. 'There are shortages of aircraft for air defense against submarines.'

"Wright said the Atlantic powers knew of these shortages be-

Naval forces, and the tactics to deal with these vital requirements of limited war, are not getting adequate funds or attention.

British observers of their own government's policy find it also over-absorbed in all-out nuclear war and dangerously deficient in developing capacity to deploy forces anywhere in the world, where vital interests may be assailed. The London *Observer* writes:

". . . it is impossible to follow the Defence debates and Ministerial statements without gaining a most disquieting impression that some Ministers are insistent on the largest possible British nuclear strike force, not to help the United States to deter Russia from war, nor even to handle Russian aggression without American aid. Its real purpose is to be able to involve America in war at our discretion.

"Mr. Sandys made the following remark in the Defence debate of April 16. 'So long as large American forces remain in Europe, and American bombers are based on Britain, it might conceivably be thought safe — I am not saying that it would — to leave to the United States the sole responsibility for providing the nuclear deterrent. But when they have developed the 5,000-mile inter-continental ballistic rocket, can we really be sure that every American Administration will go on looking at things in quite the same way?' " [25]

---

fore the exercise but that the maneuvers 'accentuated' needs in this direction." — *Washington Post and Times-Herald,* September 29, 1957.

[25] July 28, 1957.

A week later the *Sunday Times* (London) made the same point:

"A world of sovereign States, especially one riven as is the world today by acute ideological differences and rival ambitions, is ordered in the last resort by the disposal of national power. . . . And it is the ultimate power that controls the ultimate decisions. That ultimate power is concentrated today in the hands of the two giants, the U.S.A. and the U.S.S.R. If they monopolise it, the ultimate decisions rest with them alone, and with the balance of ultimate power between them. The British nuclear-weapon policy asserts in effect that it is better that this monopoly should be qualified: that by virtue of our contribution — only a contribution, admittedly, and not a large one — to ultimate power, we and our European and Commonwealth intimates should have some say in the ultimate decisions. It is a proposition hard for any good Briton or any good European to challenge." [26]

"But," says the *Sunday Times*, "there is another sense or aspect of status as a world power. It is the capacity to deploy power anywhere in the world where vital interests may be assailed. . . .

"The second aspect is still the more essential today. Indeed the paradox of the present power situation is that the more effective the ultimate nuclear deterrent is, and the more remote therefore become the chances of all-out world war, the greater the dangers of sub-nuclear warfare all round the globe. If, then, in order to retain our standing

[26] August 4, 1957.

61

as a world power in the first sense, we undermine our capacity as a world power in the second sense we are destroying our own purpose. A man pruning a tree must beware of cutting off the bough on which he sits."

Both *The Observer* and the *Sunday Times* agree that the military policy of the Conservative government, as announced in its recent white paper, would, if continued, be catastrophic to British interests and call for a change. "If this means scaling down our plans for nuclear-weapon production and development, then that is the conclusion that must be faced." [27]

The government of the United States cannot plead that it does not have the resources to develop both nuclear and conventional forces.

Nuclear Weapons in Limited War

Our Promethean punishment for having stolen the nuclear fire of the gods is not only to live with the horror of our achievement but to live with the achievements and decisions of others. It does not lie in our hands alone whether or not smaller nuclear weapons will be developed and used. What might be best suited to the interest of our coalition may be made impossible by the actions of others. But, until others do make it impossible, we can decide whether it is in our interest to rely on the smaller nuclear weapons to meet situations short of total nuclear war.

The recent Russian announcement of their success with rockets only underscores the need to push development in

[27] *The Sunday Times* (London), August 4, 1957.

this and all its related fields. For to know less or be less well prepared than our opponents could bring disaster.

But this does not answer the question of where our interest lies, nor can this be decided from what is sometimes called "a purely military point of view." This phrase is not synonymous with the best military opinion. It usually means a point of view which assumes the willingness and ability of a population to fight, and to be prepared to fight, without concern for any consequences except those which it is hoped to inflict on the enemy. It describes a method of attempting to exclude political and psychological factors from a calculation. In the choice of strategy and weapons no method is more erroneous or disastrous, since the excluded factors have a profound effect upon the political cohesion of a coalition. Whenever the protection, proferred by a leader, seems to the other members of the coalition to be more dangerous and destructive than the threat posed by the enemy, cohesion within the group will end. A friend has pointed out to me that Patrick Henry's enspiriting defiance was put in the alternative. He said "Give me liberty, *or* give me death." As a call for unity, "Give me liberty, *and* give me death" would hardly be effective. If this is the way any proposed strategy appears to our friends, it will not contribute toward a workable non-communist world system, whatever its theoretical merits from the theoretical "purely military point of view."

Whether the use of smaller nuclear weapons would help or hurt in creating a non-communist world system, holding it together, and defending it and our own interests against less than an all-out attack cannot be sweepingly decided on *a priori* grounds. Unhappily, here as elsewhere, decisions rest on facts which are varying and changing. It will simplify matters a little to consider, first, the use of these weapons in possible conflicts arising outside of Europe, and take up later on, in considering the part played by NATO in the whole strategy of a free world, the question of equipping NATO forces with nuclear weapons.

Outside of Europe military effectiveness and cohesion among non-communist states are best served by reliance on conventional forces organized and equipped to combine great mobility and fire power. Forces of this sort should be able to accomplish all that military power can properly be called upon to do in limited conflict — not to hammer an enemy into unconditional surrender, but to stop actions which are injurious to our interests.

Thoughtful criticism of our restraint in Korea does not suggest that we should have used atomic weapons in or out of Korea. It is rather that we should have struck at Chinese bases in Manchuria and sought out her newly acquired air force.[28] This, it is argued, would have led China to withdraw her forces from Korea, which was all that was necessary. I am not going to argue the merits of this criticism, or of the foundation on which it stands — that the Soviet Union would have remained passive everywhere had the suggestion been followed. Those who had

[28] See *Air University Quarterly Review*, Spring, 1957, p. 20.

responsibility for the decision thought otherwise. I mention all this to show that even in so considerable a conflict as Korea, the criticism of our conduct there — even that put forth by General MacArthur — contended not against the adequacy of conventional weapons but contended for the desirability of enlarging the geographical scope of the conflict.

It has been argued, notably in the case of China, that nuclear weapons are necessary to redress the balance in a confrontation with vast hordes of manpower. But "vast hordes" do not fight battles; only those do so who, trained and armed, are present at the crucial spot. We might still paraphrase General Forrest about the importance of getting there "fustest" with the "mostest" fire power. Furthermore, armed conflict with China would not seem to be likely in places, or under circumstances, where vast numbers would be involved. In case, for instance, of trouble over Formosa or the off-shore islands — passing over the wisdom of the policy — the use of nuclear weapons would be disastrous to our political relations. Use of such weapons, moreover, would have equally unfortunate consequences in the military operation should the Russians, anticipating our action, "lend-lease" a few nuclear bombs for retaliation on Formosa, only a hundred miles away, and on the protecting Seventh Fleet.

The wise conclusion, I believe, is that the employment of nuclear weapons, in whatever limited use of force may be necessary outside of Europe, would not be in our interest. They are not necessary to achieve the results we should desire, and their use would be harmful to the principal object of creating, maintaining, and defending a non-communist world system.

Can We Afford the Forces We Need?

The military policy which is outlined here will cost a great deal. We shall be told that we cannot afford it.[29] We never have doubted, or would doubt if we were attacked, that the United States could afford to devote whatever resources and manpower might be necessary to preserve itself. Surely, it is folly now to shrink from effort

---

[29] President Eisenhower said in his press conference of September 3, 1957, either that we cannot afford it or do not need it, or both:

"CHALMERS M. ROBERTS of The Washington Post and Times-Herald — Mr. President, Sir, in view of the Soviet Military developments, and the negative Soviet attitude on the disarmament talks, plus the inflationary problem, do you intend to attempt to keep the military budget at the $38,000,000,000 figure for the next two fiscal years, '59 and '60, as has been reported?

"A. — Well, you will recall this, that I have tried to make the difference between a new obligational authority and expenditure authority, expenditure program. I have come to believe that a very fine and adequate defense for the United States can at present prices be sustained at an, with an expenditure program, if it can be planned in advance, at about 38,000,000,000.

"Now, manifestly, there is no sacrosanct nature of any particular figure of that kind. I am talking about — of that order, in that area. I believe that as you go beyond, you get into things that are unnecessary, and if they are unnecessary, they are certainly unwise from the standpoint of the whole economy. If you go below, I believe that you are getting into an area of unacceptable risk." — *New York Times*, September 4, 1957.

and close our eyes to the crisis of the world struggle — to the opportunity which is now offered, and will not be open long, to create a non-communist world system through which our own nation, and others like and unlike it, may flourish, and have the only security available "among the sundry and manifold changes of the world."

I have said this so often that confidence in my powers of persuasion wanes, and I take the words of another. "[The nations of the Western world] have said that they cannot afford to maintain two military establishments. . . . To say this is tantamount to saying that — in contrast to the Soviet Union which continues to support two military establishments — the richest, politically and technologically most advanced, and still most powerful combination of nations on earth cannot afford to protect their interests without running the risk of universal destruction. Which is another way of saying that they cannot protect their interests at all, insofar as that protection requires the use of force.

"The truth is that financially, economically, and technologically, they can well afford two military establishments. What their leaders think they cannot afford is the political courage to demand of their peoples the sacrifices necessary to protect and promote their national interests under the condition of atomic peace. In a word: the deficit is political and moral, not economic and financial.

"With the decision to scrap traditional military establishments and arm its remnants with atomic weapons, the

Western world may well have passed the point of no return. At the end of the road that the new pacifism has begun to travel there may indeed lie peace, either the peace of appeasement and ultimate surrender or else the peace of Babylon and Carthage — the peace of total destruction." [30]

[30] Morgenthau (cited above, note 17), p. 505.

III

The Need for Strength at the Center

So, in the Libyan fable it is told
That once an eagle, stricken with a dart,
Said, when he saw the fashion of the shaft,
"With our own feathers, not by others'
hand,
Are we now smitten."

Aeschylus

We have seen that a world system, which for the hundred years between 1815 and 1914 operated as the Concert of Europe, was destroyed in our century along with the empires which composed it. Two competing systems have emerged from the ruins. The Soviet Union is the ruthless and powerful leader of one of these. The other can hardly yet be called a system. It is rather a series of groupings of nations outside the communist orbit. If these groupings are to be pulled together into a workable system, the leadership must come from the United States. No nation except the United States has the necessary strength. The task of leadership is one heavy in cost and responsibility. The United States has no acceptable alternative to undertaking it. The chief object of our foreign policy, and much of our domestic policy as well, should be to perform it successfully. We have looked briefly at the industrial productive power required, at the necessary international economic relations, and at military forces needed to protect from nuclear attack and lesser harm. But this does not exhaust the requirements to bring cohesion and strength to the nations of the non-communist world.

When De Tocqueville wrote that the American and the Russian nations seem each "marked out by the will of Heaven to sway the destinies of half the globe," he wrote also that "the principal instrument of the former is freedom; of the latter, servitude." Here, in a nutshell, we see the task and its difficulty — to lead a group of free nations by the methods of free association. Empires created by force are the oldest phenomenon in history. The Russians understand the method, as the Romans did. But where shall we find record of a coalition of free states which held together very long after a common danger seemed to fade away? Not that one cannot hold together; but to understand the difficulties will give dimension to the problem and suggest the sort of conduct which can lead to success and that which can lead to disaster. It may remind us also, to rest our hopes on the soundness of our provisions and not upon the blunders of the enemy.

The Nature of Leadership

"The essence of leadership," wrote a former colleague, "is the successful resolution of problems and the successful attainment of objectives which impress themselves as being important to those whom one is called upon to lead." And Thucydides has the Corinthian ambassador speak to the Spartans of the duties of leaders in this way: "We say their duty, for supremacy has its duties. Besides equitably administering private interests, leaders are required to show a special care for the common welfare in return for the special honors accorded to them by all in other ways."

This is the heart of the matter, the fundamental requisite of leadership. If supposed leaders do not understand this and act accordingly, they will not be followed. Because the government of the United States, in recent years, has not successfully resolved problems or attained objectives which impressed themselves as being important to our allies, it has lost the confidence of those who had looked to it for leadership. It has not seemed to them to have shown a special care for the common welfare of the non-communist community. Instead, by "agonizing reappraisals" of our policy toward Europe, by approaches to the brink of war, by a Far Eastern policy which our allies have openly rejected, by the tragic crisis over Suez, it has seemed to them to consider its own interests and objectives to the exclusion of theirs. A nation which continues to impress its allies in this way has renounced leadership and with it the goal of a workable and secure system of free states.

For me, here or elsewhere, to tell the government what it should do in the great variety of situations with which it will be confronted is foolish. No outsider has the information — though many commentators seem to think they have — or the control over the timing of action, or over the personnel through whom action is taken, to do this. I have mentioned elsewhere that Charles E. Hughes, when asked what he would say if asked to advise the Secretary of State on some current problem, replied, "I should ask for an opportunity to go through the papers." One who lacks the current and intimate knowledge of an official must speak in broad terms. What I shall try to do is to set out some of the principles by which a group of free states may be held together, and the touchstones which, when action must be through a coalition, determine whether proposed conduct is helpful or hurtful.

The Importance of Our Relations with States of the Western Hemisphere and Europe

A principle, which is as fundamental as it is disregarded, is that in the organization and maintenance of power, relations with states which are closest geographically and in interest and purpose are the most important. Primacy must be given to maintaining confidence and trust in these relations. In our case, these states are those of the Western Hemisphere and Europe. Here lies the central power which will support — if it is to be supported at all — a non-communist world system. To say this is not to minimize the importance of Asia and Africa; but if the center is not solid, relations with the periphery will not supply strength.

Obvious as this is, we rarely give it a thought in connection with the Western Hemisphere. Here we happily assume, until we are shocked by a development like that in Guatemala a few years ago, that good relations and strong societies come naturally and without effort. With clichés about our three thousand miles of undefended frontier with Canada and the good neighbor policy toward Latin America, we pass on to worry about Algerian independence and the Imam of Oman. Yet all is not going well in our hemisphere.

Relations with Canada

In Canada resentment against United States public policy and private interests has assumed considerable proportions. In large part this comes from thoughtlessness, ignorance, and bad manners south of the border. No real difficulties hover as in Europe. And so we take Canada for granted, little realizing the intensity with which Canadians cherish their country's separate identity against the pervasive influence which seeps in from the south of them. Constantly threatened with inundation, their dikes are always leaking. We think it a compliment to tell Canadians that they are just like Americans. Our economic embrace is stifling. To be sure, it has produced an unprecedented boom in Canada, but also considerable worry as to who, before long, is going to own Canadian resources and be in a position to direct Canadian economic policy. All of this calls for special thought and manners in living with a neighbor whose population, less than a tenth of ours, is as vigorous and capable as any in the world, whose geographical position and resources are of an importance which cannot be exaggerated, and whose basic interests are closer to ours than those of any other country.

Canada's two leading statesmen, of opposing political parties, agree in their concern over their southern neighbor. The Honorable Lester B. Pearson, former (Liberal) Minister of External Affairs, winner of a Nobel Peace Prize, and a good friend of the United States, has spoken with characteristic frankness:

"We know, of course in Canada — or we should know — that [our] destiny cannot be separated from that of the American people with whom we share a continent in a tense and dangerous and shrinking world. The facts of geography and geology and economics; the requirements of interdependence in the search for peace and security, tie us together, even more closely than we are both tied to others.

"It is, in fact, the inevitability and the compulsions of this interdependent relationship that give rise at times in Canada to some anxiety. It gives us a feeling, which I know we share with some other states, that we are in danger of losing control of our own decisions and our own future. True, we enjoy all the old-fashioned pride and privileges of sovereign independence. But it is also true that this sovereignty does not give us control over the decisions which determine our destiny. You have to be a super-power with a hydrogen bomb to enjoy all the attributes of sovereignty now — and perhaps not even then. . . .

"Some of these [anxieties] spring from our desire — indeed our determination — to maintain on the northern

74

half of this continent a national society which will be distinctively Canadian. We know there are obstacles — geographic, economic and social, to the fulfillment of this desire and we ask ourselves how we can accomplish it when our newspapers, our air-waves, our television screens, our magazines are so largely filled with the manifestations, especially the more exciting manifestations, of life across the border; only some of which you would want us to copy. . . .

"The possibility of American domination expresses itself also in other ways. Our natural resources are becoming more and more important to a country whose own resources are fast being depleted. In many respects, Canada is almost virginal in this field of resources and you know what happens to foolish virgins! The development of these resources in recent years — to our own as well as to your great advantage — has been assisted greatly and in a few important cases, dominated by American capital and enterprise. . . .

". . . Our prosperity, even our economic stability, depends on the maintenance of a high level of exports. That we have so far succeeded in maintaining this level is shown by the fact that today our 16 millions of people have become the fourth largest trading nation in the world. But there are difficulties and dangers ahead and these are largely concerned with our trading relationships with you. More specifically, they arise out of our growing unfavourable balance of trade across the border and out of your policies in disposing of surplus agricultural products which affect our competitive position in traditional markets.

"As to the first, the figures will explain our anxiety and our grievance. Last year, our country with less than one-tenth of your population, bought 4,167 million dollars worth of goods from the United States; more than was purchased by the whole of South America. We are by far your largest customer and we pay our bills in cash. In return, you bought 2,819 million dollars worth of Canadian products, leaving us with an adverse trade balance of $1,348 millions. Capital imports, I know, have helped to bridge that gap. . . .

"Unless our exports to the United States can be increased, Canada will obviously have to take some kind of remedial action. You will understand, therefore, our irritation and worry when our efforts to bring about such an increase meet demands here for further tariff protection against Canadian imports, already so much less than your own exports to Canada.

"The resentment caused in Canada by this process is increased when attempts are made to justify these demands for more protection on the ground that the requirements of defence make national self-sufficiency in certain commodities essential. This argument may well be valid in respect of certain vulnerable areas which might be closed to you as a source of supply in time of crisis or war. Surely it does not apply to Canada. We are the less impressed by the argument because on many other occasions we are told by other American authorities that defence can only be considered as a continental problem and dealt with on a continental basis. It is, I think, a simple, though significant, fact that any further restrictions on Canadian imports into the United States would make further defence co-operation more difficult. At least, that is how I feel about it, and I am sure you would wish me to express my feeling in plain language as is customary when Americans and Canadians speak to each other." [1]

Two months later the new Prime Minister expressed the same concern. [2]

Bad manners, also, cause trouble. The conduct of the

[1] Address before the American Society of Newspaper Editors at San Francisco, July 13, 1957.

[2] " . . . Canada has a carry-over of wheat which amounted to over 700 million bushels this year. It is vital to Canada's economy that some 300 million bushels of wheat be exported every year.

"Canada can compete for her share of the market of the world, providing other nations follow recognized competitive practices. The share of the world market for wheat by the United States has been increasing in recent years by its policies of surplus disposal, and that increase has come about mainly at the expense of Canada's export trade, which has been decreasing. The surplus disposal legislation of the United States has made it difficult, if not impossible, for Canada to maintain its fair share of the world's markets. . . .

" . . . Capital from the United States has played an important role in the development of Canadian resources. We welcome this investment and intend to provide the best foreign investment climate in the world. The heavy influx of American investment has resulted in some 60 percent of our main manufacturing industries, and a larger proportion of our mine and oil production, being owned and controlled by United States interests. . . .

"There is an intangible sense of disquiet in Canada over the political implications of large-scale and continuing external ownership and control of Canadian industries. The question is being

Senate Subcommittee on Internal Security in the case of Canada's Ambassador to Egypt, who subsequently took his own life, was, in the mildest view, excessively bad manners. The subcommittee's information regarding Mr. Norman had been told to the Canadian government. That government had investigated and retained confidence in him. Nevertheless, the subcommittee continued to cast insinuation and suspicion on a servant of a friendly government who was in no way accused of any action against this country. Resentment in Canada was strong. A few murmured apologies from the White House, a few condemnatory editorials did not mend matters.

Relations with Latin America

To the south of us live people of different and differing temperament, language, cultural tradition, and stages

---

asked: 'Can a country have a meaningful independent existence in a situation where non-residents own an important part of that country's basic resources and industry, and are, therefore, in a position to make important decisions affecting the operation and development of the country's economy?' Canadians ask that American companies investing in Canada . . . be incorporated as Canadian companies making available equity stock to Canadians. That there is cause for questioning seems clear when I tell you that it is estimated that of American-controlled firms operating in Canada not more than one in four offers stock to Canadians.

"There are other problems but time denies reference to them. What I have said is not spoken in a spirit of truculence or of petition. My purpose is to have causes for disagreement removed, which unsolved may diminish the spirit of understanding, which is characteristic of our relationship," — The Honorable John Diefenbaker, on September 7, 1957, at the Anglo-Canadian-American Convocation at Dartmouth College.

of development. Latin Americans comprise not merely the twenty-five millions of Spanish and Portuguese descent but over a hundred millions of Indian, African, and mixed ancestry. Good relations and sound policy toward these countries require more than just allowing forces already in operation to do their beneficent work, as is so largely the case with Canada. Positive action is called for by pressing problems; and a far greater effort is needed to arrive at mutual understanding and respect.

To begin with, in the two continents of the Western Hemisphere the capacity for the art of government, and the importance attached to government, are not the same. At best, government seems to pose problems for man more perplexing even than the atom. The past success of a society in the art of governing is no guarantee of its ability to meet the complexities of constitutional democracy, as the Greeks and Italians have learned. Nor does high cultural attainment give the key, as even more witnesses can testify — Frenchmen, Germans, Spaniards, and Chinese, as well as Italians and Greeks. Our Latin American neighbors have trouble with government, even more than we do. Peron and McCarthy are both signs of failure, but different failures. McCarthy signified a "degradation of the democratic dogma"; Peron, a grasping for stability through dictatorship.

I stress this point because we must not confuse good relations with the Latin American nations and the existence in each state of that representative constitutional structure envisioned in the Gettysburg Address. We have a deep and sympathetic concern in the development of representative government and constitutional restraint in Latin America, just as I am sure they and the Europeans have in its development here (their keen interest in our handling of the civil rights bill is an indication of it). Here we are on very tricky ground. By all means let our influence and, I hope, example guide and help all the American republics towards a growing capacity and fervor for representative government and the restraints of truly constitutional systems. But we must be careful not to act as the schoolmistress of the Western Hemisphere. We have a proper stake in how their governments behave toward us and affect our interests. We can properly object to infringements of them, or to conduct or to relations with our enemies or potential enemies likely to weaken the security of all of us. We can properly act to help them to participate in the life and to reap the benefits of a free world economic system. When we begin to take action, as a government, to oppose suspensions of representative government and *habeas corpus,* and to berate those responsible, we are moving out of the area of proper conduct. Here I am preaching what I have learned the hard way. To express collective indignation may bring the glow of moral principles vindicated without effort; but it is usually futile, and, more often than not, harmful.

What we may properly ask of Latin America, and what its countries may properly ask of us, can be judged by the criterion which these lectures urge as the goal of sound American foreign policy — the establishment of a work-

80

able and secure non-communist world system. Our common military problems are not, at present, complicated, and joint work is going forward. On the economic side we are, perhaps, at the end of the beginning, but not much beyond it. Why, one may ask, is economic conduct or development in Latin America a more proper concern of ours than internal political conduct there? Indeed, one might go further and inquire whether much economic development is possible without political stability and governmental effectiveness?

Of course, the condition of government, its stability, conduct, and reliability are of great importance. But, like the state of the country's resources, these factors have to be accepted as they are. Sometimes both impose severe limitations, but a great country can go forward despite considerable handicaps from its government, as France demonstrated for several centuries. In Brazil they have a saying that the country grows at night, when the politicians sleep.

Economic development in the southern continent is a basic contribution to the achievement of the great goal we have sketched; lack of it, a serious detriment. A vast population, which gains nothing from belonging to a world system, will not give it much loyalty or provide it with much strength. Some day, not too far distant, the Indian population of Latin America is going to awaken to an attitude of appraisal. It will be greatly to the interest of all of us in the hemisphere to have material progress and a wider distribution of benefits occur within the existing social framework, rather than to have them sought by its revolutionary overthrow. There are lessons to be learned here from Bolivia and Guatemala. There is reason to believe that in the hemisphere acceptance of the principles of the Bill of Rights may be best advanced by economic development and diffusing its benefits.

In a few countries — Brazil, Colombia, Mexico are in the forefront — lie great possibilities of industrial strength. Brazil has a territory greater than continental United States, resources hardly inferior — if there is petroleum in the north, as seems probable. It has not the social or racial problems which plague South Africa. Brazil, with her fifty-eight million people, and already equalling the rate of Soviet industrial expansion, is about where this country was when, after the Civil War, it entered its period of great growth. Anyone with an eye to the future should see here a partner of potential power.

If all were as simple as in Canada, the problem in these countries would be in restraining and not in supplying capital. But it is not. The uncertainties, the doubts regarding governmental composition and action, economic trends, and business standards by no means preclude, but delay, the flow of private investment. This brings the need and the opportunity for joint planning and governmental financing of facilities, essential to growth, but unlikely to attract private investment — ports, railways, water power, for instance. This was being done successfully by the Joint Brazil-United States Economic Development Commission until its abandonment. Its work went beyond purely technological, economic, and financial matters; for close personal relations were established which permitted discussion of delicate but nonetheless essential questions.

The intimate connection between the industrialization of undeveloped areas and the strength of the free world was discussed in the first chapter. It is only necessary to stress here that in our relations with Latin America courtesy and manners, as well as farsighted investment and trade policies, are even more important, if that is possible, than with Canada. The Latin Americans are inheritors of a different but old and proud tradition and culture. Understanding between them and us is not always easy. Misunderstanding and the giving of offense, unfortunately, are. To further and maintain that mutual respect, upon which alone sound relations between us can rest, each has the right to expect of the other courtesy and manners, as well as honest and fair treatment.

The Foundation of European Security

M. Raymond Aron, referring to the nations of Western Europe, has written: "Confronted with an empire which, as Mac Kinder predicted, comprises the entire 'Heartland' from mid-Germany to Vladivostok, they can survive only with the active support of America." [3] It would be true to add that so far as America, using the term in its broadest sense, is concerned an environment

[3] "Nato and the Bomb," *Western World*, June, 1957, p. 11.

in which national and individual freedom can survive and flourish requires that Europe also remain in the free world system.

The North Atlantic Treaty, its organization, and its military forces are recognition of the truth that no balance of power in Europe, or elsewhere, adequate to restrain Soviet power is possible unless the weight of the United States is put into the scales. Without association with the United States, the European powers cannot prevent the leaders of the Soviet Union from having their way in Western Europe. Without American association with Western Europe, independent national life in Eastern Europe cannot revive. Without this association, no unification of Germany, on terms tolerable to West Germans, East Germans, and their neighbors is possible.

Let us see why this is so.

In the first place, there can be no doubt that the Soviet Union has the capacity — were it not for the association of Western Europe with America — to have its way both in Germany and throughout Europe. What that would mean we can gather from the experience of Eastern Europe. Whether the rein would be looser, because of Western Europe's greater distance from Soviet borders, or tighter, because of its greater potential danger and usefulness to the Soviet Union, we need not argue. In either event it would mean Peoples' Republics of some sort, operating within limits set and maintained by Soviet force. Of Soviet capacity to bring this about — absent the American alliance — there can be no doubt.

What of Soviet intention? The Russians have been at some pains to make clear their intention to act to the limit of their capacity in determining the alignment of Europe, and especially of Germany. In Eastern Europe, Greece and Turkey, in opposition to the Marshall Plan, in the blockade of Berlin, in the meeting of the heads of government in Geneva in 1955 and of foreign ministers which followed it, in the conference with both West and East Germans in Moscow afterward, the Russians have been bluntly, even brutally, forthright. If there are any Germans, or other Europeans, who hope that the Russians do not mean what they say and do, they might ponder the comment by Thucydides on the Athenians' response to reports of Sparta's hostile intentions. "At first," he wrote, the Athenians "would not believe the charge, giving too much weight to their wish that it might not be true."

When we say that the Western European nations can survive as independent states "only with the active support of America," what exactly do we mean? We mean something very specific. We mean that the only deterrent to the imposition of Russian will in Western Europe is the belief that from the outset of any such attempt American power would be employed in stopping it, and if necessary, would inflict on the Soviet Union injury which the Moscow regime would not wish to suffer. The regime will not believe that this will happen if the United States and Western Europe are separated and stand alone. The problem of coalition policy on both sides of the Atlantic is

85

for leaders and peoples to understand this truth, act upon it, and with steady nerves run whatever risks are necessary.

So long as the United States had a virtual monopoly of nuclear weapons, the path of policy was not too obscure. The regime in Moscow, in considering action or intimidation aimed at Western Europe, knew that the vast preponderance of risk — and a lethal risk at that — had to be borne by it. This risk was posed by the Strategic Air Command. In addition, a respectable ground force in Western Europe was necessary to prevent subversion by threat, as in Czechoslovakia, or by a swift thrust from occupation troops in Eastern Europe able to break feeble resistance before bombers could reach the Elbe.

This was pretty much the original strategy of NATO. The treaty provided the political declaration of unity and will; the Strategic Air Command provided a wholly believable sanction; the unified command under SHAPE provided respectable ground forces; and, also, the presence of American troops in Europe made clear that "an armed attack against one" member of the trans-Atlantic partnership would "be considered an attack against them all." The amount of effort which the Russians have spent in trying to undermine it shows that it was not a bad strategy.

With the passing of the nuclear monopoly the problem has become more complex, involving some of the considerations raised in the last chapter. Specifically, the question arises whom, under the new situation of substantial nuclear parity, does the threat of nuclear retaliation deter, and deter from doing what?

Take two extreme situations for purposes of analysis. Is it credible that the thrust of a few East German divisions across the Elbe would be answered by a nuclear attack against either East Germany or the Soviet Union? I do not think so. The United States and its NATO allies should be quite capable of raising and maintaining in Europe forces adequate to handle a challenge of this sort. If no such forces were in existence because our allies did not wish to provide them, the thrust of the few divisions would present to the United States the issue of whether to choose that moment for the exchange of mutual destruction with the Soviet Union. Here nuclear parity is a deterrent to the United States.

Suppose, now, that a major attack is mounted against a Western Europe defended by substantial and spirited forces including American troops — an "all-out" attack, in the current phrase. Would our potential enemy believe that this would bring SAC into action? He would, I think, believe it, because of the great likelihood that it would happen. Here, in effect, he would be making the decision for us, by compelling evidence that he had determined to run all risks and force matters to a final showdown, including (if it had not already occurred) a nuclear attack upon us. Much would, of course, depend on the resoluteness of men in high places. Furthermore, because of the short time within which the decision would have to be taken, a great deal would have had to be prepared in

87

advance. This would, in turn, have been reflected in policy. The Russians, for instance, clearly understood the resolution with which this government faced the blockade of Berlin and did not, as they could have done, interfere with the air lift. In the case, therefore, of all-out attack, or in the case of raising the intensity of a smaller one, nuclear power would be a deterrent to the Soviet Union. In other words, it is a deterrent to the Soviet Union provided Western Europe and the United States maintain and have the will to use a substantial defense in Europe, capable of requiring from the Russians a major effort, as part of which they would have to weigh a nuclear attack on the United States. A defense in Europe of this magnitude will pass the decision to risk everything from the defense to the offense.

The Illusion of German Neutrality

Later the question will arise whether so substantial a defense requires nuclear weapons, but first comes the critical requirement that our European allies have the will to defend themselves. For just as the NATO allies can make it true that an attack on one is an attack on all, they can also make it untrue. It has been argued — for instance, by the German Social-Democratic Party — that NATO is a hindrance to peace, to European security, and to German unification. Hence, according to this argument, it should be dissolved, and in any event, Germany should be entirely disassociated from it. At the Party Conference

88

held in Munich in 1956 a resolution adopted contained these demands:

"The Federal Government should seek active, all-round negotiations with a view of replacing the existing bloc policy by a system of collective security;

"The Paris and Warsaw Treaties should be reviewed so as to release both parts of Germany from their military commitments and to *permit an understanding of the Four Powers on the military status of all-Germany; . . .*"

This policy, it is argued, would permit the reunion of Germany, reduce tensions and the burden of armaments, and — through a European security treaty — "guarantee" the tranquility of Europe. A policy which would produce these results would be a good one indeed.

The argument put forward can beguile only if one fails to see that it is disingenuous through the suppression of an unarticulated premise. The question it raises goes deeper than that posed by *The Economist* — how many neutrals can stand on the point of a NATO — by adding a proviso that there is no NATO. The unarticulated premise is that Germany, as a condition to unification, shall render impossible the defense of her territory and of Western Europe against Soviet penetration and domination. This would be accomplished by the dissolution of any unified forces in Europe capable of offering more than token opposition and also by the destruction of the political cohesion which creates and sustains them. Instead, the security and independence of the Western European nations would be rested on Soviet restraint and the "guarantee" of a security treaty. As for Soviet restraint, all that the Soviet regime can accomplish in Europe, without risk, it will attempt. One cannot argue with those who believe otherwise, so strong is the will to believe. But since Hungary the number of these must be small.

So we must look to the restraining character of the treaty itself and the penalties for its violation to "guarantee" the security of Western Europe. We may dismiss at once the idea that a contract, a treaty, the pledged word, would impose any restraint at all upon the Soviet government. No one who has dealt with it in regard to the Yalta agreement to establish free governments in Eastern Europe, or in the attempts from 1947 to 1950 to create a free and unified Korea, or in the Berlin blockade, or the unification of Germany, to name only a few instances, can doubt the arresting capacity of communist dialectic to establish that any action which the Soviet Union has taken, or wants to take, is not only permitted, but required, by any treaty or other form of words which may be brought up.

The "guarantee," if any, must rest in the penalties for violation of the treaty; and this brings us full circle back to the American connection. Western Europe "can survive only with the active support of America," as we said at the outset. How does the proposed policy affect the efficacy of American support? In my judgment it nullifies it, by destroying the whole foundation upon which it rests. Why is this so? Why does not the ultimate sanction, the threat of American atomic retaliation, remain as effective under a European security arrangement (whatever it may be) as under NATO?

Imagine that the European members had dissolved NATO, in a belief that it had become inimical to their interests, or that Germany had withdrawn from NATO for similar reason. In either event Europe would be left undefended by any common defense force. To dominate such a Europe would require no major effort by the Soviet Union. A move by the Soviet Union in such a Europe would be entirely equivocal from the point of view of the United States. It would not be a clear signal of a Soviet determination upon an ultimate test of strength with the West. Though a serious step, greatly to the detriment of the United States and of Europe, it would appear to most Americans, as to the Russians, as something to be expected — indeed, almost inevitable. Our withdrawal from a position once strongly held would indicate to the Russians an abandonment of any intention to dispute the position as an issue of survival. The Soviet Union will invariably probe points of weakness. A Soviet decision to move in such a situation would not mean a decision to move against the United States and should not be so interpreted. Americans and Russians alike would know this. The deterrent, the threat of thermonuclear retaliation, would have lost its credibility. It is immaterial that mischance, miscalculation, or emotion might lead to American intervention. The clarity of intention all around — on the part of Western European nations, the Soviet Union, and the United States —

the clarity essential to the effectiveness of the threat as a deterrent would have been destroyed. Its credibility lies in the realm not of words but of reality — in making it true that to overcome the NATO nations, bound together by common defense arrangements and defended by substantial military forces of all members, the Soviet Union would have to contemplate a major attack, possibly on us as well. The Soviet rulers would know that this would bring upon them American retaliation.

Importance of NATO to
Eastern European Freedom and German Unity

NATO and its common defense force are not only essential for the security of Western Europe, but without them there would be little hope for the recovery of national identity in Eastern Europe, or for safe and lasting German reunification. Surely no one can doubt that Yugoslavia and Poland would not have the degree of national independence which each has, if there were no check or restraint on Soviet power in Europe. In that case both of these countries would be as dominated as Hungary; and, while Germany might be reunited, it would be under conditions which East Europeans know by their own experience, and which West Germans must know from the experience of East Germans, are all but unendurable.

Indeed, one hears it argued that so unendurable is Soviet dominated rule in East Germany that another uprising like that of June, 1953, is quite likely, that it might involve West Germany, and, through Soviet repression, bring on a world war. To avoid this danger, the argument continues, a simultaneous Russian and American evacuation of their troops from Europe should be negotiated at once. But, under present conditions in Eastern Europe, the Soviet regime would not and could not afford to withdraw its troops behind the River Bug. As Yugoslavia, Poland, and Hungary testify, withdrawal would lead to the immediate overthrow of the Russian controlled regimes in Eastern Europe and to social changes whose repercussions within the Soviet Union would imperil the regime itself — or would be thought to imperil it. This is to the Kremlin the ultimate disaster, and to forestall it all things would be dared and done. A further process of evolution is necessary, both within the Soviet Union and Eastern Europe, before a change to more complete national identity in the latter can take place without erupting into a violence which might engulf the world. When that evolution occurs, Russian and American troop withdrawals may be possible without destroying the basis of American association in the security of Europe.

For the present it is greatly to Russian advantage to discuss withdrawal but to confine the discussion to generalities, in the manner of Mr. Khrushchev's television interview of June, 1957. Without committing the Russians, these generalities tend to weaken Western resolution. They postpone Western Germany's military participation in her own defense. They encourage British belief that the expense of British troops in Europe is unnecessary. They whet French desire to concentrate wholly on North

Africa. Whenever the discussion becomes at all pointed, the Russians can insist that by American withdrawal they mean withdrawal from all overseas bases, as, indeed, Mr. Khrushchev did say during his August visit to East Germany. In reducing American power and European security, the Soviet Union, at one stroke and without any danger of retaliation, would accomplish almost as much as a nuclear attack upon the United States.

The Soviet rulers might even go further. They might agree to ostensibly mutual withdrawal so as to get the Americans out of Europe and European bases. They would know that Soviet troops would and must return to their positions. They would believe, correctly enough, that American forces, once out, would be gone for good. For an important difference between totalitarian and popularly controlled political systems is that the latter cannot overnight reverse policies entered into with a large element of internal agreement.

The aim of the Kremlin in talking of troop withdrawals is clear enough. It is to entice German Socialists and others in Europe to undermine NATO, to separate Europe from America, and to eliminate effective opposition to Soviet power in Europe. For the West to agree to these withdrawals would be folly. But that does not prove that it is impossible. For, as Dr. Adenauer was wont to observe to Sir Ivone Kirkpatrick, it is a great pity that God limited the intelligence of man without limiting his stupidity. The stimulus to this particular folly is the temptation before all politicians to tell their people that their greatest hopes and wishes can be achieved without danger and without effort. Perhaps we can avoid this disaster by constantly telling ourselves that weakness makes oppression all but inevitable, and that retribution is terrible, but just, for a nation which in troubled times is weak and friendless when it need not be.

Are Nuclear Weapons Desirable for NATO?

To think wisely about this question, we must briefly restate some of the basic truths about the defense and integrity of Western Europe. In the first place, its defense and independence are not possible without the alliance with the United States. In the second place, the American alliance loses its protective effect without a strong combined U.S.–European defense in Europe. In the recent past both Americans and Europeans have felt the allure of a policy which would virtually dispense with local European defense and rely upon the United States "drawing a line" and announcing that, should the Russians cross it, nuclear retaliation will descend upon them. But a little reflection reveals how untenable this strategy is.

To begin with, it is quite impossible to draw any clear line which would carry conviction of our purpose to the other side. Would the line be geographical? And if so, where would it run? Would the line have to be crossed solely by foreign troops? And if so whose; Russian only, or a satellite's? Must the crossing be in force — if so, in what force? Would the reason for a crossing be a factor — for instance, alleged reprisal, as along the borders of

Israel? Would a Soviet inspired coup, arming of dissidents, etc., figure in drawing the line? Experience with the Eisenhower doctrine in the Middle East does not encourage belief in the possibility of "drawing a line."

Then again, the policy requires the United States to bear the whole burden of expense and risk, since the sole instrument of defense would be U.S. nuclear striking power, and the sole enemy target would be the United States. Finally, from the European point of view, the fate of our allies would lie entirely in our decisions without our having given any hostages — in the form of forces in Europe — to cement our interests. The confidence of Europe in our future decisions is not enough to make this possible, as our reference to British defense policy has shown. It would not be healthy to have it so.

So, once again, realism drives us toward the conclusion that the security of Western Europe by means of the American alliance requires the creation in Europe of joint defense forces of sufficient strength so that, to overcome them, the Soviet Union must face the necessity of attacking the United States. This strategy relies — for the time being, at least — upon American nuclear striking power as the ultimate restraint and control upon Soviet action — not our primary reliance in Europe, but our final reliance.

Recently a theory has been put forward which proposes to substitute for "all-out" nuclear striking power as the ultimate sanction, limited nuclear war. Under this theory long-range nuclear retaliatory power is regarded as deterring or meeting only all-out war. The protection of Europe would lie in a limited form of nuclear war conducted by highly mobile, tactically independent units operating, often deep in enemy territory, like naval task forces hunting out opposing units, and preventing enemy occupation of territory. They would not be directed against cities, industry, airfields, or communications, since these would have ceased to be important.[4]

This strategic theory fails because it is based on assumptions of fact which are not true. The weapons with which to fight this war do not exist and are not likely to exist for some time.[5] Second, it ignores the crucial importance of the air battle. If the Soviet Union were contemplating the seizure of Western Europe, and if the intervention of SAC is, by hypothesis, to be ruled out, the first effort would be to knock out NATO air and missile forces. If this could be done, the battlefield might well fall to Soviet control. NATO air and missile forces, if they should survive a surprise attack, would endeavor to remove the similar forces of the other side. If, at that point, the mobile nuclear ground forces of either side remained operable they would pick up the task of destroying their opponents, together with their lines of supply, bases, etc., in the rear. A considerable part of Europe might well be knocked to pieces by these exchanges. Furthermore, a military establishment capable of these activities would not be cheap

[4] Kissinger, *Nuclear Weapons and Foreign Policy* (cited Chapter II, note 6), p. 307, *et seq.*
[5] See Paul H. Nitze, "Limited Wars or Massive Retaliation?" *The Reporter*, September 5, 1957, p. 40.

in its equipment, nor small in manpower requirements. The need for casualty replacements, alone, would be substantial.[6]

But quite apart from its military impracticality, our allies would see at once that the proposed strategy would consign them to a fate more devastating than would compliance with the demands of the Soviet Union. The merit of this strategy, they would be told, would lie in its avoidance of "all-out" nuclear war, but it would seem to be all-out enough for them, even though designed to restrain the major participants from battering each other with hydrogen bombs. Our allies might even remind us that there is no more sound doctrine for a leader — particularly one whose leadership depends upon consent — than that he should not appear to seek safety for himself through the hazards which he urges upon those whom he hopes to lead.

So it seems plain enough that the conception of making the Western coalition strong and secure by a strategy of meeting Soviet aggression in Europe with limited nuclear warfare there has as little political validity as military. It is essentially a suggestion that the two great nuclear powers protect their homelands from destruction by agreeing that, if they fight at all, they will fight a nuclear war on European territory.

Hence we return again to the constantly repeated axiom. The efficacy of the American alliance in strengthen-

[6] King, "Limited Annihilation?" Part II of his review (cited Chapter II, note 13), *New Republic,* July 15, 1957, pp. 16, 17.

ing and protecting Europe from Soviet domination requires substantial NATO forces in Europe, including American, capable of performing two functions. The first is to stop any attack meant to probe, or which is set off by accident. The second is to face an aggressor with the necessity of moving in such force that he must contemplate an attack upon the United States, as he must know that the NATO battle, if commenced, will certainly bring SAC, or its equivalent, into Russian skies. To provoke this risk would require a recklessness in Moscow which has not been shown in the past.

The answer to the question whether the NATO defense force requires nuclear armament lies in the answer to a further question: Is nuclear armament, over and beyond SAC, necessary to provide the capabilities just mentioned?

Here again the question is not a theoretical one. Certain facts are highly relevant. Already forces defending Europe can muster nuclear power which the Soviet Union cannot overlook. American air and ground forces in Europe have nuclear weapons. Britain has nuclear weapons. In all probability France will have them in the very near future. Certainly the presence of these nuclear weapons, and the possibility that they may be added to, complicates the calculation of risks for the Russians.

The Soviet leaders understand this perfectly well and have acted accordingly. The suggestion that the defense of Europe might be strengthened through nuclear weapons has brought a barrage of threats to the European countries. The Norwegians, the Danes, and the French have all had them. The Germans have been told that if their country were used as a base for a nuclear attack it would be turned into "one big cemetery," and that whoever sought to obtain nuclear arms would run "the risk of becoming in history the gravedigger of German unity." Mr. Khrushchev added his own touch in his speech in East Berlin. In case of another war, he said, Germany would become the special target of hydrogen and atomic bombs. Britain, France, and the United States, he added, were now within the range of these weapons. "No country no matter how remote is safe." "It is exceptionally important," he concluded, "that the Germans in the West should finally understand this and should not permit such a course of events." [7] Marshal Zhukov has warned that, "By the logic of armed conflict, these [American] bases must suffer retaliatory blows regardless of upon whose territories they are located." [8] And Marshal Vasilevsky has informed the British that "atomic and hydrogen bombs . . . are particularly dangerous for countries with a small territory and a large population." [9] Russian efforts to encourage the belief that neutralism is a tenable policy for Western Europe are a good measure of the problems brought to them by any increase in the military potential of Europe, particularly nuclear potential.

[7] *New York Times,* August 9, 1957.

[8] *Pravda,* February 20, 1956 (quoted by Hans Speier in *German Rearmament and Atomic War,* The Rand Corp., Santa Monica, 1957, p. 105).

[9] *Pravda,* December 4, 1954 (quoted by Speier, p. 105).

100

Among these fearful risks and problems of vast complexity, no one can be confident. But humility, even despair, in their presence does not enable us to evade decisions. For to do nothing is in itself to make far-reaching decisions. My own conclusions are that present circumstances require substantial strengthening of American and British nuclear power located in Europe, as well as allied (including American) conventional forces and tactical air power. It would, I believe, be wiser to leave the nuclear power in American and British hands and not hasten the dissemination of nuclear weapons. We have problems enough without advancing the time — which seems to me inevitable — when these weapons will be much more widely available than they are today. The difficulties which this situation will present can be more hopefully faced when we have more of our present problems nearer solution. But it well may be that European confidence in the conduct of the American government has been too much impaired to make the wiser solution possible.

Quite as important, indeed more important, than the strengthening of allied nuclear power in Europe, is the long-range policy under which it is done. It would, I believe, be a disastrous mistake to increase nuclear power in Europe as part of our present policy of increasing our military reliance on nuclear weapons. To do this would perpetuate the danger and horror of living under the sword of Damocles. We should strengthen allied nuclear power in Europe purely as a temporary measure, while pressing vigorously with our allies an escape from reliance upon

101

nuclear weapons. The escape lies in the development of allied conventional forces capable of safeguarding Europe against attack by conventional forces. If this is done with determination, there may be, for the first time, some mutual benefit in a proposal for an East-West reduction of forces.

It is continually assumed that the Soviet Union has a vast superiority in manpower over the NATO countries. This is completely untrue. The population of the Soviet Union is 202 million; of the European NATO countries 261 million. These countries have the manpower and industrial base to provide adequate conventional forces. Their governments do not, at present, have the power to mobilize them. This is not due wholly, or even principally, to paralysis of popular will by war weariness or bewilderment in the face of vast and difficult problems. It flows in part, as in France and Italy, from the weakness of governments, which after a century of inadequacy in structure and tradition, are now asked to carry new and heavy burdens; from real loss of economic strength as in Great Britain; from an apparent dichotomy of purposes, between the need for defense and the craving for unification, as in Germany; from absorption in divisive interests as in Greece. For the present the will of these countries will be strengthened by being directed toward goals attainable as a practical matter in the fairly near future. The stiffening of nuclear defense is such a goal. It is not a sound or safe long term solution.

There may well be better responses to these immense difficulties than I have suggested. I hope so. They will be found only by facing the problems and energetically and honestly seeking solutions. If we are not willing to do this, let us at least not deceive ourselves. Let us not say that we have plans for dealing with the present world crisis, or deny that one exists.

At present we are obscuring all these problems from ourselves through a busy concentration on matters of secondary importance. For international agreements to limit the testing of nuclear weapons and various aerial and other inspections supposed to prevent surprise nuclear attack are of secondary importance. To stop or suspend the testing of hydrogen bombs needs no agreement with the Russians. Some of the proposals seem dubious, but, however that may be, they are all peripheral to the main problem. Suppose, for instance, a scheme of aerial inspection over agreed areas is set up. I suppose simple prudence would require all parties to keep their strategic bombers and missile launching stations as secret and free from observation (and from surprise attack) as possible. If we have the best inspection system and see activity on the other side which alarms us, what are we going to do? Complain about it and have an investigation and by whom? Or launch an anticipatory attack ourselves? The answer must inevitably be that we can never do more than we have the capacity to do. Our capacity in turn will depend on how we act upon the matters we have already considered in these chapters

— upon our industrial productive power, upon the amount of our production which we are willing to devote to making ourselves and our allies militarily strong and economically expanding, upon the wisdom with which we have devised military forces for the tasks they must perform, and upon our success in keeping our coalition united at the center. These are the crucial matters from which we are distracted at our peril by peripheral contests.

IV

Political Precepts for
Coalitions of Free States

*To blow and to swallow at the same time is
not easy.*
                                        Plautus.

*A wise player ought to accept his throws and
score them, not bewail his luck.*
                                        Sophocles.

*To which we may add this other Aristotelian
consideration, that he who confers a benefit
on any one loves him better than he is be-
loved by him again.*
                                        Montaigne.

So far we have considered the foundation of power, its
economic base, its military form. We have pointed out the
difficulty which faces coalitions of independent states,
each absorbed in its own problems, in organizing power
to defend and expand the benefits of a free life. Without
power the opportunity to live in freedom will not continue where it now exists. But power alone will not preserve it; there must be the desire. For some this presents
no trouble. They are the ones who believe with all their

hearts that the value and meaning of human life are found in the individual, their inheritance from the cultural tradition of what used to be called — far too narrowly — Christendom. Those who have forgotten their inheritance, except as a phrase, and those who have a quite different tradition cannot be brought to repentance by condemnation or saved by exhortation. Their only path to understanding the true worth of individual freedom is by way of their own experience.

In our dealings as a nation with the peoples of other nations we can do much to smooth this path; but not through preachments. These are useless to others and bad for us. Missionary zeal to convert philosophical heathen will distract us from a task which will do much more for both them and us — that of bringing the practice of American life closer to its professions.

This statement often pains good and earnest people who see the crisis of our century as a battle of ideas unrelated to conduct. They would burnish the ideology of freedom and with gleaming words crusade against the communist infidel. But the struggle between Christendom and Islam, which the figure of speech calls to mind, was not a struggle of words or ideas. It was a struggle of power. It would, of course, be absurd to suggest a dichotomy between ideas and power. No one knew better than those hard men, Cromwell and Napoleon, the moving force of ideas in driving men to action. None, too, knew better that the outcome of struggle is determined in the field of action.

Some years ago a gifted Irish Foreign Minister insisted

that it was my duty to devise and state on one page, and in words which would set the world ablaze, the faith of free men. I pointed out to him that the Irish temperament was far better suited to this high endeavor — though the requirement of brevity might be a hurdle — than my more mundane inheritance from the Scots lowlands, by way of Ulster, and the south of England. More than this, I offered him a quiet room and, for content and style, the Lord's Prayer, the Declaration of Independence, and the Gettysburg Address. But he had a luncheon engagement.

Beyond — but not above — the desire to keep open and extend the opportunity to live in freedom, something more is needed. It is not inspirational in nature; rather it concerns the standard by which, if freedom is to be preserved, we shape our relations with non-communist states. It deals with the long view — with what we may properly ask of these others, and they of us; with what we should expect to come from what we give; with what things should concern us deeply and what should not.

In discussing these questions I shall not, for the most part, use the language of moral discourse or invoke moral authority. Not because moral principles can, or should be excluded from the relations of states to one another. I certainly have no desire to extend the scope of Lord Melbourne's remark, "I have as great a respect for the church as any man, but things have come to a pretty pass when religion is allowed to invade the sphere of private life." It is rather because to characterize conduct between nations as moral or immoral will involve us in confusions of vocab-

ulary and of thought with which, despite their importance, we need not struggle in these chapters. The language
of moral discourse — colored as it is apt to be at one end
with fervor, and, at the other, with self-righteousness — is
more likely to obscure than clarify our discussion. And the
substance of moral discussion, which concerns the conduct
of individuals within a society toward one another, is more
likely than not to be misleading if applied to the relations
of one society to another. Undoubtedly the problems have
something in common. Morality in individual life has to
do with those restraints upon conduct which are adopted
or imposed because there are others upon whom one's conduct impinges with more or less directness and effect. So,
too, restraints upon the conduct of a society as a whole
may be adopted or imposed because of the effect of one
society upon others. But they are not the same restraints.
They deal with different situations; and it is best to state
principles in terms of their purpose and effect without
characterizing them as moral or immoral.

Nor does it help to search for a test of right conduct
in what others will applaud. People are apt to approve
what seems in their own interest. On every important issue world opinion seems to divide with the violence of the
atom. Indeed, the most serious issues among nations arise
from this division.

Perhaps we shall do better to be less ambitious, "to
elevate them guns a little lower," as Old Hickory is said
— I am sure apocryphally — to have advised his troops at
the battle of New Orleans. If we act in ways which are

helpful in accomplishing what we have to do and avoid doing what is harmful, it may be easier to find our way, however hard it may be to follow it. The task is to join with others to get a workable international system of free states. Whatever makes for the strength and unity of those who are trying to do this seems desirable; whatever weakens or divides them, undesirable. If primary importance must be given to strength and unity at the center of power — that is between us and those most closely associated with us — then whatever makes for that is especially desirable; and whatever weakens or divides us is especially undesirable.

To be more specific, what sort of conduct between us and our closest allies meets the specifications laid down? Again the requirements are simple to state, if often hard to follow. First of all, each is entitled to expect of the others loyalty to the common enterprise. The survival of all may depend on this. Essential, too, is the most candid discussion and responsible consideration of any matter deeply affecting the interest of any of the associated states. But talk is not enough. Considerable sacrifices must be made on the part of all to get common action where the vital interests of any are involved. Finally, there is hardly a more lethal blow to any alliance than to have one ally join the enemies of other allies.

The Lessons of Suez

This, in all conscience, is platitudinous enough for the most exacting taste. But I gain courage to say it from the wisdom of Terence — "Nothing is said nowadays that has not been said before" — and from the fact that within a little more than a year our coalition was brought to the verge of destruction, and may well have been permanently damaged, by violating every one of these canons of conduct. Of course I am speaking of Suez.[1] It will not help us to apportion blame, or speculate upon who made the first error, or why men acted as they did. Folly was contributed by all concerned too generously and continuously to make this easy or useful. Suez and its tragedy provide a clinic in the inevitable results to a coalition of conduct which violates the principles which we have outlined.

If this sorry episode is put into perspective, by looking at it from the distance which time gives, what stands out? First, three nations, without whose close concert of action the Western coalition and a free world system cannot hold together, were divided on a matter of great importance; second, each side regarded as disastrous to its

[1] Suez had its ominous antecedent in the Indochina collapse of 1954. I shall not go into the details. The resultant effect of our action upon our alliance is well described by Mr. Edwin Tetlow in his comment on Mr. Drew Middleton's book *These Are the British:*
" . . . He says, for example, that Britons felt Mr. Dulles let Sir Anthony Eden and the Foreign Office do the donkey work in patching up European unity in 1954 and negotiating a settlement in Indo-China. The Secretary of State and the Administration were ready to take a share of the credit for success but were only too eager to remain aloof from failure. Mr. Middleton coldly observes that such a policy of limited liability in great affairs is not in accord with either the power of the U.S. or the principles preached by Mr. Dulles and others. One feels that even the Foreign Office couldn't have put the point more dispassionately — or more effectively." — *Saturday Review*, August 17, 1957, p. 20.

own interests, and to the interests of all, the outcome which it suspected the other side of being willing to accept; third, neither side was wholly candid with the other. At length, when one side, through desperation and folly, took action of great hazard to all and of doubtful outcome, the other joined in defeating and humiliating it. This is the barebones of the matter, and neither talk about the United Nations Charter,

" . . . nor all your Piety nor Wit
Shall lure it back to cancel half a Line,
Nor all your Tears wash out a Word of it."

The long reluctance of the British government to accept the abrogation of the 1936 treaty with Egypt and give up its Suez base rested on the conviction that this water route to Middle Eastern oil, and to Commonwealth countries which lay to the east, was a vital interest which it would not, without a fight, permit to fall under the arbitrary power of another state. Colonel Nasser's forcible seizure of control of the canal raised this issue acutely and under circumstances which suggested that Mr. Dulles's abrupt withdrawal of financial help for Egypt's Aswan dam was a substantial cause. Some of the most powerful members of the British government made it clear to our government that they were prepared to fight rather than give in. But at a later stage the British government did not inform ours of its plans to use force. It is fair to go further and say that, at that stage, its conduct was deceitful.

111

The French were concerned only with any action which would overthrow Colonel Nasser; otherwise they saw no end to their troubles in Algeria. They made no secret of this. It was always obvious that the French would use force if they could get the British to join them. What would happen would pivot on British action.

On the American side, it now seems quite plain that the government was prepared to accept what the British would not accept — Egyptian control of the canal with only such concessions to appearances as could be wheedled out of Colonel Nasser. It would not join in or tacitly approve the use of force to counter the Egyptian move, but would vigorously oppose its use. It would make no inconvenient sacrifice of attitude, relations with others, or funds to help the British. This was not made crystal clear to the British. Indeed, it is fair to say that in the London conference and in the episode of the Canal Users Association our conduct, whatever the intention may have been, led to expectations which proved to be false.

In this situation the British, believing that the protection of their interests must lie in their own action and that the Arab-Israeli war offered a favorable opportunity to act, secretly joined with the French in an expedition to seize the Suez Canal zone. This was foolish in conception and execution. The expeditionary force was not constituted to be able to seize the canal quickly before it could be damaged; nor had the consequences of damage been

112

accurately foreseen. The force was not strong enough, nor the British public determined enough, to have occupied Egypt against continued resistance and the condemnation of the non-communist states. If the effort bogged down in possession of a damaged canal and with Colonel Nasser still resisting, there was no plan of what to do next. The sole strategy rested on the mistaken belief that, with the destruction of his air force by bombing and with a threat of landings, Colonel Nasser would be deposed and his successors in power would make a satisfactory settlement of the canal issue. With the very best of luck, the enterprise required speed and dash. It was marred by irresolution and delay. The unexpected developments in Hungary had a bearing on this, for Britain and France were fearful of finding themselves cast in the same brutal role as the Soviet Union.

At this juncture the Russians made threats that volunteers would join in the battle in Egypt and rockets would bombard Britain and France. The United States government, with its "loins girt about with truth, and having on the breastplate of righteousness" — as St. Paul admonished — joined the Russians and the Arab-Asian bloc in raising the hue and cry against its friends. Under this pressure Sir Anthony Eden and M. Mollet collapsed; and Colonel Nasser was "able to quench all the fiery darts of the wicked" and don the "helmet of salvation."

Conduct such as this between allies would have

113

strained any alliance to the breaking point, regardless of what was involved in the controversy.[2] But when the matter at issue was the route to Middle Eastern fuel, without which the whole industry of Western Europe was in deepest trouble, the damage struck in two directions. Our allies were taught that, not only would we make no sacrifice to help them in a matter of vital interest, but that we would join the opposition to them. The Middle Eastern states discovered that their bargaining power with their European customers was enhanced, since no matter what they did to the property or rights of others, they would not be restrained by force.

It is not for an outsider to say to governments what course they should have followed, particularly here where almost any course would have been better than what eventuated. The field for choice was broad. The public affront to Colonel Nasser in offensively cancelling the

[2] "Recent events have been the most humiliating in the history of American diplomacy. So distrustful of the United States had Britain and France, our closest and oldest allies, become that they did not inform us of their projected attack on Egypt. . . . It is impossible to imagine a more inept diplomacy; it is incredible that the United States should have maneuvered so clumsily that it was forced into such an intolerable situation. It may be that our vote against the British and the French has helped our position in Africa and Asia, our moral position, that is. But if we are to defend Europe against Soviet aggression or subversion, we can do it only with the aid of Britain and France. The administration knows this so well that it is now asking our allies to forget what has happened. Well, one can only hope that they will be magnanimous." — Bernadotte E. Schmitt, "Dilemmas of American Diplomacy," an address before the University of Tennessee Chapter of Phi Kappa Phi, January 28, 1957.

offers of financial aid was avoidable. While in the summer of 1956 there did not exist the force necessary to seize the canal undamaged and to hold it until Colonel Nasser's arbitrary act — and perhaps the Colonel himself — was repudiated, it could by energetic common action have been ready by the autumn. Even active United States participation in this was not — to use a current and silly word — unthinkable, and might have been salutary had the need for it developed, which I doubt. Participation in the preparation would have had effect enough. The possibilities of subsidizing — where useful for Western interests — a boycott of the canal, or a blockade of it, were not explored because they involved substantial cost. The opportunities for economic pressure on Egypt were great as were the longer range pressures from developing water uses in the upper Nile, and of increasing Western Europe's bargaining position both with the oil producers and Egypt by alternate power, large oil storage, large tankers for the longer route. To believe that the Western allies were so powerless here, that they must end by weakening their own alliance in their collapse seems to me quite untenable.

Of course, the Soviet Union would have blustered, threatened, and made all the propaganda value it could out of a really strong and united stand by the Western allies. But the Soviet Union was having troubles of its own in Hungary. Indeed, the way it met those troubles may give us pause for thought. When the Kremlin concluded that the Hungarian revolt threatened its vital interests, all other considerations became secondary. The

115

revolt was crushed. This act of brutal conquest, unsurpassed by the conquistadors at their most ruthless, is rightly condemned by all who dare to speak. But thought should not end with condemnation. We should understand that the free world faces a regime with the capacity to decide what infringements of interest cannot be permitted, and to act on the decision. This is a quality of the utmost importance. All decision sacrifices something. It sacrifices the courses of action not chosen, and the approval of those who do not like the decision. But nothing could be more true of the leader of a coalition than another sentence of St. Paul's — "if the trumpet give an uncertain sound, who shall prepare himself to the battle?"

The Problem of Blowing and Swallowing at the Same Time

Of course, it will be said that I am talking the language of imperialism or colonialism, or both, and that a policy of maintaining strength and unity at the center of the free world, as of first importance, will antagonize Asian and African peoples who, if we look to the future, should weigh more heavily with us than Europe. The charge, I believe, is untrue, but it does raise all the difficult problems of our relations with the vast numbers of hitherto dependent peoples, newly come to manage their own affairs and those who aspire to do the same. The problem is all the more tangled because the experience of these peoples which has made the words imperialism and colonialism so bitter in their mouths has been with our

116

European allies. The dialectics of the various disputes finds much that is apposite in our own early history and polemical writings. Finally, these people have not experienced, as have the Baltic and Eastern European peoples, imperialism in the Russian style; they have little tradition of individual liberty; and they are rightly impressed with the strides which the Soviet Union has made toward industrialization, but are without knowledge of what they have cost. Americans, caught between the necessity of preserving our coalition with European nations and the desire to be influential with the new nations of Asia and Africa, have been learning how difficult it is, as Plautus said, "to blow and swallow at the same time." It is of some help, though not much, to think out what our relations with these new nations may properly be.

To begin with essentials, it is greatly to the interest of the West that Africa, the Middle East, South and Southeast Asia, and Japan shall remain in an open world system and not be absorbed, economically and politically, into the system organized and led by the Soviet Union. But, if this is to occur, it must, also be to the interest of the Asian and African peoples, and appear clearly to be so. The pull of political and philosophic ideas alone will not be enough to create this interest; and nationalism generates more suspicion of the West than of the East. Most of these peoples do not know, as the Poles or Hungarians could tell them, what happens to national independence once a people have fallen within the orbit of Russian power. However much Asian leaders might want to keep

117

free from any foreign domination, including Russian, they will not be able to do so — for they will not remain in power — unless they are able to make progress with economic development. To do this they must get help or adopt authoritarian methods. If help does not come from participation in a free world economic system which provides for it, it will come from the communist system.

I have discussed all of this earlier. It is pointed up as I write by two developments. One is the failure of both the executive and legislative branches to understand the nature and importance of this essential part of foreign policy. The apathetic way in which a hodge-podge of foreign subsidies, called the "foreign aid bill" was presented to Congress led one Congressman to express the general opinion of that body in this way: " I would support any program that would assure gradual withdrawal of expenditures for foreign aid but I am unwilling to approve . . . the present program . . ." [3] The other development is India's growing plight.

To allow Mr. Nehru's and Mr. Menon's unusual gifts of causing annoyance to blind us to the importance of India and the need for rapid economic development there would be a great mistake. If Mr. Nehru did not exist, our greatest hope for India would lie in inventing him; for he, alone, seems to have a fair chance of holding India together while economic development lays a foundation for social and political stability. His most trying utterances,

[3] Representative Will E. Neal (R., W. Va.), 85 Cong., 1 Sess., *Congressional Record,* 103: 13434 (August 14, 1957; daily edition).

118

like those we make in this country, are for domestic consumption; and his foreign policy, as was ours during our early history, is a function of India's experience and of the heavy pressures of Indian politics.

All these are minor; the central point of concern to us is that the new Indian state shall succeed as a free state in an environment of freedom. Should it fail, disintegrate into confusion, collapse economically, as Indonesia seems to have done, the catastrophic consequences for Asia would be hard to exaggerate. The nub of India's problem is plain to see. India's first five-year plan was well conceived, well executed, and an economic success. Production expanded rapidly and, most remarkable of all, per capita income increased for the first time in half a century.

The expansion was not rapid enough to bring political success. Unemployment and underemployment were not decreased; political criticism of the Congress Party was increased, the communists gained control of government in the State of Kerala, and made headway elsewhere. Mr. Nehru responded, as President Roosevelt responded to Huey Long, by moving to the left. He put forward a "Socialist pattern of life" for India; and insisted on expanding the development program. But here the parallel may stop. For, increasingly, the effort appears to be too heavy for India to carry without more and more totalitarian control — or the help of foreign capital. Indeed, it is not unlikely that some of those who urged the expanded program would be quite content with the former. So far as

119

Mr. Nehru is concerned, it is hard to see that he had much choice.

Here, then, is the essence of India's — and Mr. Nehru's — plight. The United States and Europe, as well, have an interest, hard to overstate, in helping to solve it. There is nothing difficult about doing so. What that involves is capital assistance on a loan basis; India will not accept grants. The West has the funds and plenty of industrial capacity to turn out the equipment required. What seem to be lacking are understanding of the urgent necessity and the will to act.[4]

[4] "WASHINGTON, Sept. 7 — India is seeking $1,000,000,000 in loans from Western sources in the next three years, Indian officials here said today.

"Unless the Government of India can borrow substantially this amount, these officials said, it may have to abandon some of the most essential projects in its second five-year plan of industrialization, and postpone many more.

"These officials are at pains to delineate the nature of the Indian financial crisis. The Indian economy, they say, is fundamentally sound and potentially wealthy. The present foreign exchange difficulties have been brought about by heavy investments in wealth-producing capital goods, and not by import of luxuries.

"But they frankly state their belief that India is now at a turning point in her effort to raise the standard of living and achieve a self-sustaining national growth through a mixed economy. . . .

"Two days ago Prime Minister Jawaharlal Nehru said in an interview in New Delhi that India would welcome a United States loan of $500,000,000 to $600,000,000.

"The Indian Government hopes it can obtain the remainder of the needed $1,000,000,000 from Britain and from further loans from the International Bank for Reconstruction and Development and private banks." — *New York Times*, September 8, 1957.

120

The Indian economic situation has been worth stress‑ ing as an opportunity to do, in relation to an Asian coun‑ try, something which is both quite possible and also vital to the grand strategy of our foreign policy. A matter of this sort should concern us deeply. Matters of a different nature should not. I refer to such things as pulling the eagle's tail feathers, Indian claims to a moral rectitude rarely achieved in this imperfect world, and even policies which do mischief, as I believe Indian policy did in the Suez crisis and is doing in Kashmir.[5] In the latter case we made our best try toward a solution by appealing for a reasonable and conciliatory approach. But it was made clear that power was to be the decisive factor.

To countries still in the agricultural state we can give help to hasten their emancipation from it. This help will have to be a gift. Most of these countries have no com‑ modities with which to pay; and for those that have, the proceeds of what they can sell are, from every point of view, best invested in their own development.

At once, it will be said that I am oblivious of what

[5] A typical minor sample:
"NEW DELHI, Aug. 23 — Moroccan Foreign Minister Ahmed Balafrej today said his country would like the United States, France and Spain 'either to get their troops out of Morocco or arrange con‑ ditions for temporary stay.' The United States maintains four large air bases in Morocco.

"The Foreign Minister, who is here on a visit, said he found In‑ dian Prime Minister Nehru in sympathy with his views. He also said his talks with Nehru ranging over other subjects had been 'satisfying'." Reuters dispatch, *Washington Post and Times-Herald,* August 24, 1957.

should be the true objective of United States policy in this part of the world, as revealed by a Senator in a speech in the Senate on July 2, 1957. The true objective, he said, was to gain for these nations freedom from Western imperialism. The Senator spoke also of the danger of Soviet imperialism. But this seemed to concern only Eastern Europe. His example was Poland; his recommendation, the laudable one of lending the Poles money. However, nothing so simple would meet the "challenge of imperialism," which the West presents, in the spot most "critically outstanding today — Algeria." To meet this challenge, he believed, was "the single most important test of American foreign policy."

The Senator spoke quite correctly of the great harm which the Algerian struggle was doing both in France and Algeria, of its repercussions everywhere, of the fact that, if reason governed, solutions were not beyond the wit of man. (This is true, also, in Kashmir, which was not the subject of the Senator's speech.) He upbraided the State Department for shilly-shallying; proclaimed his devotion to "our oldest ally," and her importance; then popped his solution, a resolution:

". . . the President and Secretary of State . . . hereby are strongly encouraged to place the influence of the United States behind efforts, either through the North Atlantic Treaty Organization or through the good offices of the Prime Minister of Tunisia and the Sultan of Morocco, to achieve a solution which will recognize the independent personality of Algeria and establish the basis for a settlement interdependent with France and the neighboring nations; and be it further

"*Resolved,* That, if no substantial progress has been noted by the time of the next United Nations General Assembly session the United States support an international effort to derive for Algeria the basis for an orderly achievement of independence." [6]

The requirement for orderliness is the supreme touch of naiveté. Once again, within a year, the United States would join the enemies of her oldest ally to force that ally to an American conception of proper conduct — though this time, at least, we would give her some advance warning; for the General Assembly was then still eleven weeks away. Of course, it would all be for her own good; and whatever happened in North Africa or to the Western alliance would be insignificant, for we should triumphantly have met "the single most important test of American foreign policy today," the "challenge of imperialism."

Nothing could be more injudicious than this proposal, except making it. That act has contributed to the difficulty of solution in Algeria. The Senator should have known that he was not telling intelligent Frenchmen anything they do not know. What he does not understand is the humiliating agony of the loss of power and position. One does not need a crystal ball, either in France or here, to foresee the outcome in Algeria; but the adjustment of a society to loss takes time. It will not help for us to snap impatient fingers

[6] 85 Cong., 1 Sess., *Congressional Record,* 103: 9718-9726 (July 2, 1957; daily edition).

123

at a people who were great before our nation was dreamt of, and tell them to get on with it. It will do immeasurable harm. In all likelihood France will need help in solving her troubles. It will be a great pity if the Senator, and others, disqualify us from the role of helpful friend. There is no remote possibility that his speech can advance solution.

I wish the Senator could have been with me a little over five years ago at a meeting on this very subject at the Quai d'Orsay. It was held at the request of the French government and attended by most of the cabinet and four or five former Prime Ministers. The meeting was a long one. The first part was taken up with a bitter complaint that the United States was undermining France in North Africa, voiced in turn by nearly all the French participants, and a blunt request was made to know what we wanted. Was it to remove French influence from North Africa?

For a full hour I laid the situation out, completely and frankly, saying everything that the Senator has said and a good deal he has not thought of. I explained why the American democracy — they had complained especially of the press and radio, speeches in Congress, by labor leaders, and clerics — always took, and always would take, the side of any people who seemed to be underdogs, oppressed by foreign intruders. To their complaint that our public was ignorant of the full facts of French-North African relations, I pointed out that popular discussion was always carried on in broad strokes. No responsible person in or out of the American government, I said, wanted to remove or weaken French influence in North Africa. It was essential from every point of view — economic progress, social stability, military security. But the problem which France posed for her friends was that she was faced by a rapidly deteriorating condition and had no policy for dealing with it. I spoke of the inevitable outcome of drift. We would back any policy which offered even a small hope of success; the better the policy, the more enthusiastic our support would be. If they wished to consult with us in devising one, we would assume the responsibility which that involved. In any event, I could not conceive of any American government — and at that time, I could not — which would join those whom France regarded as bent on her destruction.

The air was cleared. For another hour or more we discussed the matter in mutual confidence. But the solution came no closer. They were quite frank that past policies were inadequate; they were working on new ones; they were confident that all would be put right; but, at present, there were serious political obstacles. All of us on the American side of the table left the meeting deeply saddened. It was plain to us that in the fading of the French position in North Africa this group of highly intelligent and patriotic Frenchmen saw farewell, a long farewell, to all French greatness. The road ahead led inevitably to a conclusion which, as yet, Frenchmen were too divided in will and too emotionally involved to face. The course, even for one utterly detached who knows that he cannot stop and cannot usefully hasten the inevitable conclusion, to say nothing of a friend deeply concerned for the renaissance of that French vigor of mind and spirit which is irreplaceable in a world of free men — surely, the course for neither is to plunge in his dagger with the rest.

But, it will be said — indeed, the Senator has said it — that, sad as this may be for France, we must capitalize the inevitable and make friends and be able to influence people. But it is an illusion that we shall gain either friends or influence. If anyone was ever saved after he had sunk for the third time it was Colonel Nasser, but if he has either friendship or respect for his savior, it is not noticeable. The United States cannot gain in North Africa at the expense of France. Association with France is essential to North Africa, as no one knows better — or says more frankly — than President Bourguiba of Tunisia. If France and all Frenchmen were pulled out tomorrow, bag and baggage, we would soon be more reviled than France ever was. For the departure of France would reveal all the more starkly to the Arabs their two implacable enemies, as they are now revealed in Tunisia — their own incredible fecundity and the desert. They would fight them, as Colonel Nasser does, by identifying them with the West.

No, I do not believe the Senator's speech, or the attitude it represents, holds promise of anything but harm in our foreign relations.

Perhaps one great advantage of the age which has passed was the slowness of communication. So much becomes unimportant if one does not know about it for months or years. How one envies Mr. Jefferson's calm complaint to the American Minister in Madrid that he had not heard from him for two years, and his hope that this would be remedied before another year was out. But now the press, like a busy cupid's messenger, brings all the gossip, foolish words that wound, as well as wise ones which inform. "I lay it down as a fact," said Pascal, "that, if all men knew what others say of them, there would not be four friends in the world." No one can say that statesmen and press together are not making progress toward this result.

Problems of Policy Presented by Political Blocs

Another mistake which a leader of a coalition should avoid is worth brief mention. This is to be forced by pressures of domestic politics into a fixed position on a specific point of foreign policy. It is, of course, obvious to all of us that the domestic problems and attitudes of a nation are among the factors determining its foreign policy. Jingoism, for instance, has its appeal. It was this which led Richard Cobden to say, "Palmerston likes to drive the wheel close to the edge, and show how dexterously he can avoid falling over the precipice. Meanwhile he keeps people's attention employed, which suits him politically. . . ." [7] Pacifism has, perhaps, an even stronger appeal. In two of our elections all candidates ran on their promises to keep us out of war. Let us hope they believed them at the time. The extent to which a people can be brought to see the

[7] Philip Guedalla, *Palmerston* (G. P. Putnam's Sons, New York–London, 1927), pp. 467–468.

127

values of the long view, and sacrifice for them, is always the ultimate limiting factor. It is not to all this that I am referring.

The point is a much narrower one. It concerns the adoption of a specific attitude toward a particular country because the pressure of specific blocs makes it expedient. One cannot score partisan advantage here. The finger can be pointed at both parties; at the Democrats, for too great compliance with voting pressures in their policy toward Palestine; at the Republicans, for a China policy deeply bent by purposeful pressure blocs. The damage lies in the fact that the nation, which should be the leader of the Western coalition, is so immobilized, by reasons unconnected with the effect of a policy upon the welfare of the coalition that it cannot lead. This weakens the coalition.

In the case of our present China policy a number of pressures — some of them motivated by specific pecuniary interest, others by the emotions created by the attack on the last Administration, some by a curious love-hate involvement with China — have prevented us from making a calm analysis of the facts in the Far East and the courses open to us. An organization, "The Committee of One Million," moves into action the moment an appraisal is suggested. The action of Congress in accepting, blindly and with hardly a word of question or debate, the Administration's 1955 treaty with Formosa and legislation to further it, is an example of this uncritical submission to dogma. It is time to pause and ask ourselves some questions.

Why are some of us so obsessed with China? Why does

128

our government seem so much more belligerent toward the communist regime in Peiping than toward the far more sinister one in Moscow? We have always given China romantic importance. Now we tend to think of it as a far more dangerous and powerful enemy than it is. "What constitutes power in our time?" asks Mr. Nathaniel Peffer. "Clearly it is constituted of population, resources, accumulated wealth, industrial structure, scientific knowledge and technological advancement. Of these properties what has China?"[8]

He answers that neither now nor "in the easily measurable future" has China "the foundation for a great military Power."[9] Her large area and manpower give her defensive but comparatively little offensive strength. They also contain sources of weaknesses; for, unlike Russia, China is overpopulated, undernourished, has no untapped agricultural lands, no substantial agricultural exports to provide buying power abroad. Her resources are meager, compared to those of the Soviet Union or the West. Her industry small, backward, despoiled in Manchuria, and destined to a laborious struggle by lack of means to acquire the necessary materials and equipment for expansion. Despite all state-directed efforts, electric power production is still less than a fourth of Canada's and steel an eleventh of Russia's, which, in turn, is less than half of ours.

China is not a slightly more retarded Soviet Union.

[8] "China in Reappraisal: Menace to American Security?" *Political Science Quarterly,* December, 1956, p. 490.
[9] *Id.,* p. 491.

In Mr. Peffer's words, "Her strength is derivative. She now and for many years can serve only as transmission belt for Russian military power." [10] That power at second remove can be stopped, as it was in Korea, if, as discussed earlier, we have the sort of forces which can deal with it; and, also, provided there is complete solidarity in our coalition. But this is exactly what we do not have, and will not have, so long as we pursue a rigid policy which was not made and is not discussed from the point of view of the national and coalition interests it is supposed to serve, or of the dangers which it may involve.

A fair rule of thumb to measure a particular foreign policy is to consider where it would take us in, say, ten or fifteen years. This was one of the critical functions which General Marshall confided to the Policy Planning Staff when he created it in 1947. If, here, we ask ourselves where our present course toward China will take us in fifteen years, or by the death of Chiang Kai-shek, whichever comes first, some questions call urgently for answers.

In the first place, is our present policy of supporting, economically and militarily, the Nationalist Government as the government of all China, against the communist regime, likely to remain acceptable to Americans or to Formosans who believe that they have any choice about their future. The United States' treaty commitment is a limited one. We have not annexed Formosa, or established it as a military base for American forces. The treaty can

[10] *Id.*, p. 492.

be cancelled on a year's notice, and its provisions are far from specific. The support of Formosa costs us, annually, about one-third the amount of the New York State budget. In fifteen years it could cost from a third to a half of the whole Marshall Plan.[11] If Quemoy should be attacked, its only effective defense would be by general war with China; and perhaps intermediate-range rockets have already made this true of Formosa, also. The present Chi-

[11] "Despite repeated all-island surveys by teams of competent American experts and endless conferences among high Nationalist officials, the fact remains that this is an Alice-in-Wonderland economy. It is made unreal by Nationalist ambivalence as to whether Taiwan should be developed as an independent unit or integrated into a reconquered mainland. As the hope of rewinning China fades this becomes less important, but no corresponding cut in military investment results.

"The unreality is perpetuated by the general assumption that whatever the deficit, American assistance will meet the difference. Although domestic politics in the United States is beyond the scope of this study, failure to consider this aspect would leave our analysis two-dimensional. The Nationalist Government has very strong supporters in the United States. For example ICA officials in Taiwan have even found their requests for appropriations raised in Washington because of American political pressure responding to pleas for support from Nationalist circles. Nationalist confidence that politics will prevail where economics fails lowers the incentive for them to utilize their resources most effectively. . . .

"Chiang Kai-shek's regime requires a large annual subsidy indefinitely, perhaps diverting assistance from critical countries such as Indonesia which last year received one-tenth Taiwan's economic assistance for a population eight times as large." — *The United States and the Far East,* background papers prepared for the use of participants and the Final Report of the Tenth American Assembly, conducted under the auspices of the Graduate School of Business, Columbia University, November 15–18, 1956, pp. 183, 195.

131

nese defenders of the island are the same troops, for the most part, whom the communists defeated on the mainland; but now ten years older.

It is not a prospect to inspire confidence in the United States or in Formosa. No one is likely to believe that present arrangements will stretch on indefinitely. Indeed, their temporary nature is underlined by Mr. Dulles's statement that communism in China is a passing phase.[12] Perhaps. But the phrase is equally applicable to the regime on Formosa.

Have we adequately appraised the possibility that, under these circumstances and as time goes on, some on the island might think it better to bargain with the mainland while they still had bargaining power, and that we might find ourselves defending people who did not want to be defended? Have we discounted the possibility that enough votes might be found to install the communist Chinese delegation, instead of the Formosan delegation, as China's representative in the United Nations? In that event we certainly would be charged, as we have been in the past, with fomenting revolution and aggression against another state, just as we charged others in the cases of Greece and Korea. The votes clearly would be stacked against us.

Looking at our policy from another point of view, does it strengthen and unite our coalition? The answer seems to be that it clearly does not since our European

[12] See "Our Policies Toward Communism in China," Address by Secretary Dulles before the International Convention of Lions International, San Francisco, June 28, 1957, *State Department Bulletin,* July 15, 1957, pp. 91, 95.

allies are not in agreement with it, and important Eastern nations — notably Japan — are increasingly restive.

Are there important American interests being served by our policy? Certainly not any interest in a military base, for Formosa is not used as that now. And to deny its use to an enemy is not worth much, since vantage points for an enemy aiming at Japan, Korea, or the Philippines are more available and effective than Formosa. A Chinese communist base on an island, with which water communications can be interrupted by submarines, has no advantage (and distance gives none) over bases on the mainland.

Is loyalty to an ally involved? Certain loyalties are undoubtedly involved. Persons who have worked with the United States or who have relied upon its promises cannot, in honor, be turned over to their enemies or abandoned to their fate. But it is false to identify Chiang Kai-shek or the regime on Formosa with "China" — once an allied state. As individuals they are entitled to our support and protection; as a regime or state they have no proper claim beyond the terminable legal contract. Also there are questions of the prestige of the United States among nations to be considered. But these require calm and unemotional analysis. A possible loss of prestige should not inhibit a change of policy, if continuation of the policy is likely to bring about a greater loss of prestige.

Finally, we owe it to ourselves and our allies soberly and frankly to weigh the possibility that in so incendiary a situation a spark at any time could start a blaze; and the blaze might sweep far beyond the control of anyone.[13] In this situation our closest allies see that, while ruin may engulf them, we are precluded by American domestic politics and pressure groups from the sort of consultations and adjustments of policy which may be in the interest of all.

These lessons from our own experience show us something of the conduct which is needed from us, beyond the creation of power, to make possible a buoyant and expanding life in a world of free states. They teach the necessity for strength and unity among the closest

[13] That the sparks are not lacking is shown by the following dispatch in the *New York Times* of July 18, 1957:

"QUEMOY, July 17 — This island is changing from a defense outpost to a forward command post, a high Chinese Nationalist military leader said yesterday.

"Maj. Gen. Yin Tien-chia, chief political officer of the island command, said that Quemoy was being prepared for use as a stepping stone toward the mainland.

"He said the training program was being revised in accordance with the island's new status. He did not disclose what other changes were necessary to switch from defensive to offensive tactics.

"During the last twelve months, the fortifications of the island have been strengthened impressively. Everywhere the eye can reach, cement has replaced packed clay, new roads have been built and old roads reinforced."

"The United States," writes Dr. Bernadotte E. Schmitt (cited above, note 2), "encouraged the Nationalist leader to send large garrisons to the off-shore islands of Quemoy and Matsu, which had been lightly held, and to the Tachen Islands, which had not been held at all. By way of analogy, suppose that at the end of the Civil War the remnants of the Confederate army had been able to retire to Staten Island and Martha's Vineyard. It is not surprising that the Chinese Communist government reacted violently and began to talk about attacking the coastal islands as a preliminary to an invasion of Formosa."

allies at the center of power; the futility of trying to blow and swallow at the same time; the catastrophic result when one ally joins the enemies of the others; the possibility and importance of helping in the development of the states — even though they may criticize, irritate, and hamper us — who are needed in, and who need, the free world system. Whatever benefits we may confer are conferred to further the great goal which we are seeking; and we should know very well that our concern for their success will be greater than their gratitude to us. This is right and proper on both sides; the mutuality of benefit rests on a more solid base than emotion. Nowhere is it more true than in foreign relations that the tongue "is an unruly evil, full of deadly poison," nor more needed the admonition, "keep well thy tongue and keep thy friend." Finally, just as a mental bloc may destroy the effectiveness of an individual's conduct, a political bloc may do the same for a nation.

V

Conclusion

With as much objectivity as it is given to me to achieve, I have tried to state the facts of the world in which our nation lives and deals with other nations, the role of leadership which it could so usefully play, if the civilization we have inherited is to go on, and something of how we should play it. Perhaps what we do is less important than how we do it. "What one lives for may be uncertain," writes Lord David Cecil of Conrad's view of life, "how one lives is not . . . Man should live nobly though he does not see any practical reason for it, simply because in the mysterious inexplicable mixture of beauty and ugliness, virtue and baseness in which he finds himself he must want to be on the side of the beautiful and the virtuous." [14]

Objectivity does not require one to become a cybernetic machine or involve the total exclusion of the subjective view. If the reader finds a tinge of dogmatism in what I have said, I remind him of Montaigne's words, "I should not speak so boldly if it were my due to be believed." If

[14] *The Fine Art of Reading* (The Bobbs-Merrill Company, Inc., Indianapolis–New York, 1957), p. 183.

dogmatism there be, I hope that it has not appeared as belief in the possession of superior knowledge or wisdom or as impatience with error, ignorance, or a limited outlook. These may destroy us, but, in face of the vast complexities surrounding us, they are the normal frailties of man.

On one thing only I feel a measure of assurance — on the rightness of contempt for sanctimonious self-righteousness which, joined with a sly worldliness, beclouds the dangers and opportunities of our time with an unctuous film. For this is the ultimate sin. By representing that all is done which needs to be done, it denies to us the knowledge that we are called upon for great action; and denies to us, too, the chance to "give a sample of our best, and . . . in our hearts . . . feel that it has been nobly done."